HEALING DECONSTRUCTION

AAR

American Academy of Religion
Reflection and Theory in the Study of Religion

Editor
David E. Klemm

Number 03
HEALING DECONSTRUCTION
Postmodern Thought in Buddhism and Christianity
edited by
David Loy

HEALING DECONSTRUCTION

Postmodern Thought in
Buddhism and Christianity

edited by
David Loy

Scholars Press
Atlanta, Georgia

HEALING DECONSTRUCTION
Postmodern Thought in Buddhism and Christianity

edited by
David Loy

© 1996
The American Academy of Religion

Library of Congress Cataloging in Publication Data
Healing deconstruction : postmodern thought in Buddhism and
    Christianity / edited by David Loy.
        p.   cm. — (AAR reflection and theory in the study of religion ;
    no. 03)
    Papers originally presented at the fourth International Buddhist-
Christian Dialogue Conference held at Boston University, July–Aug.
1992.
    ISBN 0-7885-0121-6 (cloth : alk. paper). — ISBN 0-7885-0122-4
(pbk. : alk. paper)
    1. Postmodernism—Religious aspects—Christianity—Congresses.
2. Postmodernism—Religious aspects—Buddhism—Congresses.
3. Christianity and other religions—Buddhism—Congresses.
4. Buddhism—Relations—Christianity—Congresses. 5. Derrida,
Jacques—Congresses. 6. Deconstruction—Congresses. I. Loy,
David, 1947–   . II. International Buddhist-Christian Dialogue
Conference (4th : 1992 : Boston University) III. Series.
BR128.B8H35 1996
230'.046—dc20   96-6921
                                                                 CIP

Printed in the United States of America
on acid-free paper

CONTENTS

Introduction

DAVID LOY

The book you hold in your hands is a confluence of two contemporary developments, both with important implications for religious thought. One is Buddhist-Christian dialogue, which has grown to become perhaps the most fruitful of many interreligious encounters today. In the 1980's a series of three conferences brought together a core group of scholars and practitioners who decided to form the Society for Buddhist-Christian Studies in 1987; one of the contributors to this volume, Roger Corless, was a founding member of that Society. Earlier versions of these papers (with the exception of Morny Joy's) were presented at the Fourth International Buddhist-Christian Dialogue Conference, held at Boston University July-August 1992 and jointly co-sponsored by the Society for Buddhist-Christian Studies and the Boston Theological Institute. One reason this ongoing, multifaceted encounter continues to be successful is that it has taken place on the level of practice as well as scholarship, and both concerns are reflected in the essays that follow.[1]

The second development reflected here is postmodernism, in this case particularly the deconstruction of Jacques Derrida, whose textual approach has religious implications that are still just beginning to be explored. Deconstruction as an intellectual fad seems to be waning—as it must, given the disproportionate attention devoted to it in recent years—but its challenge to logocentric thinking continues to spread, albeit more

---

[1]All the contributors have shown a deep appreciation for both traditions, an appreciation which is not only intellectual but the fruit of religious commitment and practice. For details, see the *Notes on Contributors* which follows the papers.

quietly, into many specialized fields, some of them quite remote from Derrida's own philosophical and literary concerns.

One of the fields most influenced has been religious studies. For some time, Derridean deconstruction has been taken to reinforce the modernist critique of transcendence which proclaims the Nietzschean "death of God" and celebrates this by dancing on his grave. More recently, however, this appropriation has become suspect for too easily accepting the anti-spiritual commonplaces of our *Zeitgeist*. It is becoming more evident how a deconstructive approach may also be employed to challenge that understanding as reductionist. John Caputo, for example, has argued for what he calls the "armed neutrality" of *différance*: armed because it holds all existence claims suspect, yet ontically neutral because it neither implies nor excludes the existence or non-existence of any entity.[2] Instead of pounding another nail into God's coffin and refuting the possibility of religious experience, then, deconstruction may provide a new way to approach those issues. An important point which keeps recurring in the following essays is that Derrida's own deconstructions open up paths that he himself has been unwilling or unable to explore. Perhaps the most important of these, in the eyes of the contributors, is the possibility of a "leap" from theory to practice which Derrida has not undertaken and which is better exemplified in religious disciplines. The dialogue has much to offer both sides: while deconstruction sensitizes us to the ways our spiritual search has become fixated on an idolatry of self-presence, the long and rich traditions of religious thought have something to teach deconstruction about the textual idolatry that *theoria* encourages when it remains divorced from a more holistic *praxis*.

So, and as one has come to expect with a volume about postmodern thought, the title *Healing Deconstruction* is intentionally ambiguous. On the one side, it emphasizes the healing possibilities of deconstruction in a field where the deconstructive turn has too often been understood reductively. The papers that follow demonstrate some alternatives to that. On the other side, the title also refers to the potential healing power of this dialogue for deconstruction itself, whose critique of logocentrism has led to a rupture within contemporary thought. What Nietzsche's Zarathustra said of man, that he is "a rope across an abyss", applies to much of postmodernism as well, for we have yet to realize what possibilities await us beyond that rupture—or rather, within that abyss.

---

[2] "Mysticism and Transgression: Derrida and Meister Eckhart" in *Derrida and Deconstruction*, ed. Hugh J. Silverman (Routledge: New York and London, 1989), 24. This essay is discussed in my paper.

Naturally, the papers incorporate and respond to postmodern themes in different ways. The feminist concerns in Berry's and Joy's essays supplement each other, and there is a deep parallel between Corless's and mine, which reach the same conclusion about the liberating power of de-essentialized religious images and concepts.

Corless's title "Idolatry and Inherent Existence: The Golden Calf and the Wooden Buddha" reflects the symmetry he discovers between the two traditions. Christianity and Buddhism both employ images and concepts, while cautioning that they may become obstacles to salvation or liberation; both teach about giving them up at a "higher" level, yet warn that their absence may also be an obstacle; and therefore both find ways to bring them back but in a new fashion: deconstructed and at the same time left intact.

To demonstrate the Christian critique of idolatry, Corless uses the paradigmatic story of the golden calf, and to present the Buddhist critique of inherent existence (*svabhāva*, self-existence) he refers to the famous Ch'an story of Tan-hsia T'ien-jan burning a wooden Buddha. According to Gregory of Nyssa, the incident of the golden calf is as much about concepts as images, for the divine can be realized only in the way Moses experienced it on the mountain, in a "dark cloud" where the understanding does not reach. *The Cloud of Unknowing* also encourages the spiritual seeker to abide in this darkness, for, as St. Basil declared in the fourth century, anyone who says he *knows* God is "perverted"! Corless compares this with the Buddhist refutation of inherent existence and particularly with the Mahāyāna deconstruction of Buddhahood, which leads Nāgārjuna to assert that we cannot say either that the Buddha exists or that the Buddha does not exist. To emphasize the parallelism between these critiques, Corless supplements his paper with an appendix that juxtaposes the supposed anti-Buddhist negatives of the *Heart Sutra* with the supposed anti-Christian negatives in the *Mystical Theology* of Pseudo-Dionysius.

Yet this deconstruction of images and concepts is not the end of the matter for either religion. Their elimination entails the incorrect view of nihilism in Buddhism and the denial of the incarnation in Christianity. So a means is found to bring them back again without falling into the opposed extremes of eternalism and idolatry. Instead of cataphatic spirituality as merely preliminary to apophatic spirituality, or there being an unresolvable tension between them, Corless argues for what he calls their co-inherence. For Christianity, he discusses this in terms of the iconoclastic controversy (fifth through seventh centuries), a debate unwittingly repeated by the reformers of the 16th and 17th centuries. For Buddhism, he discusses Nāgārjuna's understanding of śūnyatā as no-thing rather than nothing, which exemplifies Mahāyāna ontology generally: concepts need not be, in fact should not be, rejected completely, but rather reinstated once we have realized their essencelessness.

The final result of this fascinating parallelism is that Buddhism teaches the co-inherence of saṁsāra and nirvāṇa, while Christianity understands the person of Christ as the co-inherence of divinity and humanity.

If Corless's paper explores *différance* in Buddhist and Christian teachings, mine discovers *dissemination* in the writings of some of their exemplary teachers. No aspect of Derrida's own writing has been more controversial than the dissemination implied by his argument that meaning is always an open ensemble of unstable structures, whose possibilities are unlimited and unlimitable. Derrida's readiness to demonstrate this as well as talk about it has inspired less-skillful deconstructors and less-tolerant critics. "Dead Words, Living Words, and Healing Words: The Disseminations of Dōgen and Eckhart" argues that such playful, aware-ful dissemination did not begin with Derrida, and discusses its role in the texts of perhaps the greatest Japanese Zen master and perhaps the greatest medieval Christian mystical writer.

The paper begins with Caputo's claim that *différance* does not settle the God-question one way or another but rather *un*settles it, because it exposes the conceptual problems that bedevil such debates. Buddhism agrees with this and in fact carries it a step further: for what needs to be unsettled is not the God-question or Buddha-question but our "commonsense" everyday world, riddled as it is with unconscious ontological committments. According to Mādhyamika, our taken-for-granted world is mentally-constructed by our delusive attribution of self-existence to objects, which makes us experience that world as a collection of discrete things interacting in space and time; and that leads to suffering insofar as we understand ourselves too to be such self-existing things, who are nonetheless subject to the ravages of time and change—who are born only to fall ill, grow old, and die. Merely by subverting such ontological claims, and without offering any views of its own, the Buddhist deconstruction of such self-existence (especially our own) can allow "something else" to shine forth.

What does that imply about language? Buddhists have often understood it as a "filter" that should be eliminated if we want to experience the world more nondually, but that dualism just perpetuates the problem. An alternative view is hinted at by Ch'an master Yün-men: "There are words which go beyond words. This is like eating rice everyday without any attachment to a grain of rice." Dōgen's and Eckhart's writings demonstrate how words can go beyond words.

Both figures are so esteemed that we tend to overlook how opportunistic, indeed unscrupulous, their writings are. They have no qualms about twisting and even contradicting conventional teachings when it serves their purposes: in Dōgen's case, in order to devise neologisms that leap out of the dualistic ways of thinking we are stuck in; in Eckhart's case too, to develop new expressions, especially ones which can help us see through the duality between ourselves and God.

If both exemplify the linguistic freedom that Derrida has more recently celebrated, which is not pious of traditional teachings and produced effects but is ready to challenge them all, then what is the difference between what Derrida is doing and what they are doing? The answer is complex yet it may be summarized, in part, as follows: Derrida's deconstructions are naturally more concerned with the fixations that operate within language, while Dōgen and Eckhart offer broader critiques of attachment which form part of a more holistic practice that develops and extends nonattachment into all our activities, and is therefore able to deconstruct the most problematical duality of all, that between the sense-of-self and the world it finds itself "in".

In contrast to the parallelisms between Christianity and Buddhism explored in Corless's and my papers, the next two essays explore their complex relationship with a wide range of postmodern thinkers, especially feminist ones. In "Sky-dancing at the boundaries of Western thought: feminist theory and the limits of deconstruction", Philippa Berry argues that in order to transform the dominant dualism and secularism of Western thought, Derridean deconstruction needs to engage in a closer dialogue with French feminist thinkers who have already begun to address the relationship between spirituality and what Derrida has described as "the end of man". Her paper considers what that end of man might mean if we view it in relation to the concerns of Vajrayana Buddhism.

In patriarchal society woman is often associated with otherness, and sometimes represented as a disturbing nothingness. But the concept of womanhood also partakes of that *in-between-ness* which simultaneously undoes binary oppositions and maintains them. French feminist thought has been criticized for its essentialist conceptions of woman, yet its most important thinkers have developed sophisticated accounts which build upon Nietzsche's misogynist remark that "there is no essence of woman, because she diverts herself, and is diverted from herself." Berry discusses Julia Kristeva's psychoanalytic account of *abjection* as what disturbs identity, system, order—categories that include the narcissistic ego which both Christianity and Buddhism also bring into question—and she also considers new feminist versions of flight and angelic identity in Helene Cixous and Luce Irigaray.

One of the formative dualisms of Western culture has contrasted woman as body to man as disembodied mind. In the Vajrayana tradition of Tibetan Buddhism, *prajñāpāramitā*—the perfection of transcendental knowledge or insight—became personalized into a goddess who came to represent the paradoxical *embodiment* of enlightenment: the body is by definition *śūnya*, empty and illusory, yet also/and therefore dynamic, associated with spiritual energy. The same qualities are also present in the *dakini*, a feminine "sky-dancer" playing in the Void. Such de-essentialized images invite the practitioner to make a comparable leap in consciousness, cutting (*vajra* means diamond) through the obstacles to liberation. This echoes the choric aspects of Kristeva's *chora*, even as the imagery of fire in Irigaray's *Speculum* provokes analogies with the mystic fire and flame-aura of the *dakini*. The practitioner's spiritual encounter with the *dakini* leads to a purification that does not abolish negativity but integrates the pure and impure visions, the heart-body and the mind-spirit.

The story of Padmasambhava's initiation by the chief of the *dakinis* exemplifies how the body is both *śūnya* and at the same time the means of enlightenment. In Vajrayana literature such encounters with the feminine principle function as the final stage in the practitioner's search for wisdom; experiencing insight into her essentially empty nature is the most notable way one becomes a Buddha. By embracing a figure who seems opposed to earlier Buddhist teachings, then, Vajrayana attains a union of theory with practice that Western thought has not. Berry concludes that this meditative practice achieves a "dancing on the abyss" which postmodern thought today dreams about but has yet to realize.

Morny Joy's "Mindfulness of the Selves: Therapeutic Interventions in a Time of Dis-solution" explores the contemporary intersections of several fields usually pursued separately: deconstruction, Christian process thought and Buddhism, but also feminism and ecology. At issue is the formulation of a new world-view which can help us redefine the identity of both women and men, as well as their relationship with our deteriorating environment. In all these fields the question of the self has become paramount, and this common quest for a new definition of self enables us to see the interconnections among them.

Joy appreciates the postmodern decentering of the subject, yet argues that the tactics of deconstruction lead to indefinite conclusions which do not meet our needs. Ecofeminism reveals the relationship between the domination of women and the domination of nature, but has been unable to decide whether gynocentric values are the solution to such domination or are themselves a construct of patriarchy.

One of the more interesting attempts to address these problems is Catherine Keller's *From a Broken Web* (Beacon, 1986), which offers a predominantly Christian approach to process thought. As usual in process philosophy, the challenge is to balance the increasing complexity of its evolving components within a harmonious whole. Keller sees this as particularly pertinent for women because process thought avoids the extremes of separation and solubility (her terms) that have pervaded Western notions of the selves of men and women, respectively. Keller tries to avoid the common problem with process thought—that it eliminates otherness in the name of a monistic whole—yet Joy finds her process-feminism also unable to provide a satisfactory model for the interconnections she seeks betwen the various parts and the whole: the boundaries begin to blur as Keller's participatory mysticism tends to absolve all difference. Process thinkers usually try to correct this by opting for either transcendent or immanent ordering principles, to end up somewhere on a sliding scale between self-affirmation and selfless mystical absorption; but a metaphysics of presence and substance props up both ends of this ladder.

Joy finds the most promising candidate for a new world-view, and a new definition of identity, in Buddhism. She presents the central Buddhist doctrine of *pratītya-samutpāda* as explained by Joanna Macy in *The Dharma of Natural Systems: Mutual Causality in Buddhism and General Systems Theory*. Although all the fields discussed imply commitment to an informed participation in order to change the social fabric, only Buddhism requires us to change the very nature of our perception of the world by developing constant daily awareness. The historical mistreatment of women in most Buddhist institutions and societies, and the insensitivity to racism in many Western Buddhist groups today, bring us full circle to remind us that a system of checks and balances is necessary where the concerns of each field can serve as corrective for the others.

The first Buddhist-Christian Dialogue Conference in 1980 led to the formation of the North American Theological Encounter Group, which has met regularly since then. One of the key issues addressed in this working group has been the relationship between the Buddhist concept of *śūnyatā* "emptiness" and the Christian notion of *kenosis* "emptying". The major Buddhist spokesman in this discussion has been the Japanese philosopher Masao Abe, who as an important representative of the Kyoto School has for many assumed the role that D. T. Suzuki formerly filled explaining Zen to the West. In a recent paper "Kenotic God and Dynamic Sunyata" (in *The Emptying God*, eds. John Cobb and Christopher Ives), Abe has offered a detailed account of their relation, which focusses on the workings of sameness and difference as they operate within the Christian trinity. In accordance with the traditional paradoxes repeated endlessly in the prajñāpāramitā literature ("A is not A, therefore it is A"), Abe argues that both God and *śūnyatā* function in a similarly paradoxical fashion: God/*śūnyatā* is not God/*śūnyatā*, and because God/*śūnyatā* does not affirm itself as God/*śūnyatā*, God/*śūnyatā* is really God/*śūnyatā*.

There are, of course, different ways to understand this apparently contradictory logic. One interpretation is implicit in several of the other papers, most clearly in Roger Corless's essay. As we have seen, his approach deconstructs images and concepts to reveal their *śūnyatā* lack of inherent existence; rather than being rejected altogether, however, they are re-introduced as "empty" images-beyond-images and words-beyond-words. The prajñāpāramitā sutras make the same maneuver. The Diamond Sutra, for example, says there are no sentient beings, because they have no inherent existence, yet this does not eliminate them: we end up with de-esentialized sentient beings. This means, however, that there is no real paradox, for the logical contradiction is only apparent. The sentient beings of the first statement ("there are no sentient beings...") are ontologically different from those of the last statement ("... which is why there are sentient beings"). This raises questions about Abe's paradox and the way he uses it to understand the trinity—questions explored in the final paper, Robert Magliola's "In No Wise is Healing Holistic: A Deconstructive Alternative to Masao Abe's 'Kenotic God and Dynamic Sunyata'".

Magliola's book *Derrida on the Mend* (Purdue University Press, 1984) was the first, as far as I know, to draw attention to the striking parallels between Derrida's deconstruction of essentialist metaphysics and the Mādhyamika deconstruction of *svabhāva* self-existence. It made a key distinction between what Magliola termed the Buddhist "centric" or Absolutist tradition, which is still logocentric, and the "differential" critique of that tradition best exemplified by Nāgārjuna. Here he uses that distinction to criticize Abe's paradoxical understanding of god/*śūnyatā*. As Richard Robinson noticed, there are no paradoxes in Nāgārjuna's *Mūlamadhyamikakārikā*, or, for that matter, in the whole of the prajñāpāramitā. Paradox is a cosmeticized, disguised logocentrism because it attempts to be congruent with itself (in principle it encloses all its subject-matter) and because it is non-rational (as opposed to differential mysticism which is neither rational nor nonrational but "off-rational"). Magliola offers a different understanding of the trinity, which utilizes the maneuver of "pure negative reference" found in Nāgārjuna and Derrida.

The Council of Florence (1438-9) affirmed that "everything is one" in God "except where an opposition of relationship [*relationis oppositio*] exists", which means that the three persons of the trinity can be defined only by the relationships that exist among them. Following Karl Rahner's interpretation of *relationis oppositio*, Magliola understands the first person as the begetter, the second as the begotten, and the third as the passive spiration. The only maneuver which can accommodate this conciliar provision is pure negative reference.

Magliola explains negative reference with a close reading of some passages from Derrida. Like Nāgārjuna's *pratītya-samutpāda* ("dependent-coarising"), writing too is dependence-only, which therefore never achieves totality, any self-closure; and writing is just a Derridean emblem for life—all of life goes on as dependence-only. This contrasts with Abe's understanding of God/*śūnyatā* as a "Dynamic Nothingness" that is still an absolute unity, ineffable yet centered. Because Christianity is familiar with that type of rhetoric, in the final analysis Abe's view is too comfortable, too safe. Instead, Christianity needs to learn that which is *unsafe*: "that 'God' is sometimes frighteningly *impersonal* and that this *impersonality* double-binds into Divine personality in erratic, ever-altering ways that *do not* close into unity."

True healing is accomplished by negative differing, not by seeking the self-same.

The five papers in this volume use different vocabularies and address different problematics, so it is striking that they independently reach similar conclusions: the liberating and healing potential of de-essentialized concepts and images, language, bodies and symbols. Roger Corless demonstrates how Buddhism and Christianity both deconstruct images and concepts, and then bring them back, simultaneously de-essentialized and left intact. My paper explores *dissemination* in Dōgen and Eckhart, who not only celebrate the freedom of meaning but use it to devise new expressions that can help us see through the dualisms we are stuck in. Philippa Berry relates the feminine embodiment of enlightenment in Vajrayana Buddhism with the feminist concern to revalue our devalued bodies: the body of the goddess is, like ours, *śūnya* empty but also/and therefore the dynamic means of enlightenment. Morny Joy shows how the central Buddhist doctrine of *pratītya-samutpāda*—which offered the first deconstruction of self in history, as far as I know—can contribute to a world-view that heals the opposition between the sexes, as well as that between between nature and us. Robert Magliola uses the pure negative reference of Nāgārjuna and Derrida to de-essentialize the three persons of the trinity and teach us that liberation involves embracing difference, not seeking an elusive and delusive self-identity.

The other common theme, explicit or implicit in all the papers, is that actually realizing this healing potential requires a move from theorizing to practice, for only that can truly deconstruct the self. Berry finds Derrida's marginalization of French feminist thinkers "symptomatic of the male thinker's failure to convert deconstructive *theoria* into a healing *praxis*". Joy explores the contemporary interactions of several seemingly-disparate fields, all of which imply a commitment to change the social fabric; yet she finds that only Buddhism, with its emphasis on constant daily awareness, leads to a change in the way we actually perceive the world. My paper argues that the deconstruction of self-presence must be extended beyond written texts to deconstruct the "text" that constitutes our sense-of-self and the way that self lives "in" the world—which is precisely what religious practice does, or can do.

Idolatry and Inherent Existence

THE GOLDEN CALF AND THE WOODEN BUDDHA

ROGER CORLESS
DUKE UNIVERSITY

> Zhaozhou said, "A metal buddha cannot go through the forge. A clay buddha cannot go through the water. A wooden buddha cannot go through the fire."
>
> —*Blue Cliff Record*, Case 96[1]

Both Christianity and Buddhism employ images, but each tradition warns that images may be obstacles to liberation or salvation, and each teaches a level, usually said to be a higher level, at which images are given up. However, both traditions also warn that the absence of images may itself be an obstacle, perhaps even a greater one, and find ways to re-introduce them. This article will examine the use and abuse of images in Buddhism and Christianity, and propose that both traditions show evidence of an attempt to maneuver themselves towards a similar stance of images-beyond-images, in which images are simultaneously deconstructed and left intact.

IMAGES AS OBSTACLES

In Christianity, the misuse of images is called idolatry. In the Bible, the best known story of idolatry is found in Exodus 32, where the Israelites are represented as sinning against God by setting up an image of a golden calf.

---

[1] Quoted in *Moon in a Dewdrop: Writings of Zen Master Dōgen*, edited by Kazuaki Tanahashi (San Francisco: North Point Press, 1985), 254, note 9.

According to the story, Moses was called by God to ascend Mount Sinai in order to receive God's commandments. He built an altar to God at the foot of the mountain, left the people in charge of Aaron and Hur, and told them to wait. Forty days and forty nights (and seven chapters of Hebrew) later, the people understandably had grown restless and bored. Aaron agreed to a liturgical festival, manufactured a golden image of a "calf"[2], and the people proclaimed "Israel,...here is your God who brought you here from Egypt!" (EXOD. 32:4[3]). When Moses eventually returned to the Israelites' camp "[h]e seized the calf they had made and burned it, grinding it into powder which he scattered on the water, and made the Israelites drink it." (EXOD. 32:20).

In the context of the *Sitz im Leben* of the Book of Exodus, there was perhaps merely a problem of disloyalty, a group in competition with that of Moses, which desired its own image,[4] but according to the Jewish and Christian theological traditions, the fault was that an invisible, atemporal, bodiless God was mistaken as visible, temporal, and embodied. In the New Testament interpretation, we find St. Paul explaining that humans, "While they claimed to be wise, in fact they were growing so stupid that *they exchanged the glory* of the immortal God *for an imitation*, for the image of a mortal human being, or of birds, or animals, or crawling things" (ROM. 1:22–23; italics in original). Paul claims that idolatry results in immorality:

> That is why God abandoned them in their inmost cravings to filthy practices of dishonouring their own bodies—because they *exchanged God's truth* for a lie and have worshipped and served the creature instead of the Creator, who is blessed for ever. Amen. (ROM. 1:24–25).

St. Athanasius, on the other hand, in his treatise *On the Incarnation of the Word of God*, says that idolatry is *the result of* wickedness (*ek kakias*), and is due to humans "thinking of nothing more than appearances" (*mēden pleon tōn phainomenōn logizomenoi*).[5] Nevertheless, whichever way the

---

2 *ʿêghĕl* literally means "(bull-) calf", but it is conjectured that the original image was of a full-grown bull, a common symbol, then and now, for a strong and masculine deity, and that the editors have trivialized it by making it immature and sexually impotent. Cf. Ps. 106:20: "They exchanged the glory of God for the image of an ox that eats grass."

3 Biblical quotations are from the *New Jerusalem Bible*.

4 See note 32b on this passage in the *New Jerusalem Bible*.

5 Athanasius, *De Incarnatione Verbi Dei*, 11. See also sections 1, 4, 5 and 12. My translation from the bilingual edition of Robert W. Thomson, *Athanasius: Contra Gentes and De Incarnatione* (Oxford: Clarendon Press, 1971), 135 and 160)

causation is supposed to go, both Paul and Athanasius regard idolatry as, to use Whitehead's term, misplaced reification.

Misplaced reification also appears to be the point of the famous Zen story of the burning of a wooden Buddha.

> When Tanka (Tan-hsia T'ien-jan, 738–824) of the T'ang dynasty stopped at Yerinji of the Capital, it was so severely cold that he finally took one of the Buddha-images enshrined there and made a fire with it in order to warm himself. The keeper of the shrine, seeing this, was greatly exercised.
>
> "How dare you burn up my wooden Buddha?"
>
> Said Tanka, who looked as if searching for something with his stick in the ashes, "I am gathering the holy śarīras in the burnt ashes."
>
> "How," said the keeper, "could you get śarīras by burning a wooden Buddha?"
>
> "If there are no śarīras to be found in it, may I have the remaining two Buddhas for my fire?" retorted Tanka.[6]

This story can be, and has been, interpreted in many ways and on many levels. For our purposes, we may note that when the body of a real, flesh-and-blood, Buddha is burned, one expects to find indestructible relics known as *śarīras*, which one would then place in *stūpas* for veneration. Since no *śarīras* were discovered subsequent to the burning of the wooden Buddha, Tan-hsia had demonstrated that the image was manifestly not a real Buddha even though, having been enshrined in a Chinese Mahāyāna temple, it had been accorded the respect due to a real Buddha.

However, the story is not really about mistaking a wooden Buddha for a real Buddha. D. T. Suzuki is perhaps influenced by the Biblical language of his intended western audience when he says "So Tanka (Tan-hsia) burned a wooden image of Buddha to make a fire, and idolatry was done away with."[7] It is doubtful that even the most devout worshipper regarded a wooden image as a flesh-and-blood person. D. T. Suzuki is more helpful when he quotes the comment of Ts'ui-wei Wu-hsiao on this incident: "Even when [the wooden Buddha] was burned, it could not be burned up".[8]

---

[6] D. T. Suzuki, *Essays in Zen Buddhism (First Series)*, edited by Christmas Humphreys (New York: Grove Press, 1961; first published by Rider, London, 1949), 330.

[7] D. T. Suzuki, *Essays in Zen Buddhism (Third Series)*, edited by Christmas Humphreys (London: Rider, 1970; first published 1953), 347.

[8] D. T. Suzuki, *Essays (First Series)*, 331.

What is at issue here is not the location (or, better, locatability) of Buddhas, but the location or locatability of Buddha-*ness* (*buddhatā*, often translated as Buddha Nature). If the wooden Buddha had left *śarīras* behind, it might have been mis-taken as the visible, temporal and bodily (physical) home of invisible, atemporal, bodiless pure mind or reality-as-it-is. This is not precisely the same as "idolatry" in the Christian tradition—it is *svabhāvavāda* or essentialism, the belief in inherent existence—but it is similar to idolatry in that it is, also, misplaced reification. This is put clearly in Zen Master Dōgen's famous reference to the realized person: "When he meets a buddha he kills the buddha".[9] Dōgen calls this "going beyond buddha" (*bukkōjōji*[a]) and "not-buddha" (*hibutsu*[b]):

> He is not-buddha merely because he is going-beyond-buddha. "Not-buddha" is so called because buddha's face is dropped away, buddha's body and mind are dropped away.[10]

BEYOND IMAGES

So, we might ask, what was Moses *really* doing all that time on Mount Sinai? According to the allegorical *Life of Moses* by St. Gregory of Nyssa, he wasn't just taking dictation, he was going beyond words and living "in a state beyond nature", during which the people "like a little child who escapes the attention of his pedagogue, were carried along into disorderliness by uncontrolled impulses" and lapsed into idolatry.[11]

Gregory makes much of the fact that, as Moses approached Mount Sinai, there was a noise which got louder and louder, then a cloud shrouding the mountain in thick darkness. By going through the noise and fearlessly entering the darkness, Moses went beyond words and beyond sight and—

> entered the invisible things where…while not being seen, he was in the company of the Invisible. He teaches, I think, by the things he did that the one who is going to associate intimately with God must go beyond all that is visible and (lifting up his own mind, as to a mountaintop, to the invisible

---

[9] Dōgen is quoting the Chinese master Fa-ch'êng. *Moon in a Dewdrop*, 206.
[10] *Moon in a Dewdrop*, 206.
[11] Gregory of Nyssa, *The Life of Moses*, translated by Abraham J. Malherbe and Everett Ferguson (New York: Paulist Press, 1978), 46 (and see also note 101 on p. 155).

and incomprehensible) believe that the divine is *there* where the understanding does not reach.[12]

Spiritual progress, indeed, is, for Gregory, from light to darkness, from seeing to not seeing, to a "seeing that consists in not seeing" so that,

> [as] Moses grew in knowledge, he declared that he had seen God in the darkness, that is, that he had then come to know that what is divine is beyond all knowledge and comprehension, for the text says, *Moses approached the dark cloud where God was.*[13]

And this means that the story about the golden calf is not, for Gregory, really about a golden calf, but about the idolatry of concepts, for "…every concept which comes from some comprehensible image by an approximate understanding and by guessing at the divine nature constitutes and idol of God and does not proclaim God."[14] Thus, the Christian mystic is, as the author of *The Cloud of Unknowing* puts it, "to abide in this darkness" with "a privy pressing upon this cloud of unknowing"[15] for, as Pseudo-Dionysius tells us, "It [i.e., God]…is beyond every limitation", even beyond darkness itself.[16]

All this begins to sound very Buddhist. Where is the buddha that was burnt? A buddha must be different from an ordinary being, otherwise the word would be meaningless, and there could be no such thing as the Dharma, the doctrine taught by buddhas. But, when Śākyamuni Buddha asks his disciple Subhūti, in the Diamond Sutra, whether he, Śākyamuni Buddha, has taught anything, and whether he can be distinguished from ordinary beings, Subhūti replies "No, indeed, O Lord". Yet, someone is there, and something has been said. Therefore,

> "…those thirty-two marks of the superman which were taught by the Tathagata, they are really no-marks. Therefore are they called 'the thirty-two marks of the superman'".[17]

---

[12] *Life of Moses*, 43. Parentheses and italics in original.

[13] *Life of Moses*, 95.

[14] *Life of Moses*, 96.

[15] *The Cloud of Unknowing*, chapter 9. Quoted in the version edited by Evelyn Underhill (London: Stuart and Watkins, seventh edition, 1970; originally published 1912), 89–90.

[16] *The Mystical Theology*, chapter 5. Quoted from the edition of Colm Luibheid, *Pseudo-Dionysius: The Complete Works* (New York: Paulist Press, 1987), 141.

[17] *Vajracchedikāprajñāpāramitā-sūtra*, 13d. Quoted in the translation by Edward Conze, *Buddhist Wisdom Books* (London: Allen and Unwin, 1958), 52.

Nāgārjuna says:

> The Tathagata is not the (aggregation of the) *skandhas* nor is [he] different
> from the *skandhas*. He is not in the *skandhas* nor are the *skandhas* in him. As
> he cannot possess the *skandhas*, what actually is he?[18]

To cut to the chase, the answer is—

> As the Tathagata is empty of inherent existence, it cannot be asserted that,
> after liberation, the Buddha either exists or does not exist.[19]

—and, therefore, the concept "buddha" is a provisional designation or
fudge-term (*prapañca*) which must be used in order to say something but,
if it is reified, "one cannot see the Tathāgata".[20]

From this standpoint, the series of apparently anti-Buddhist
negatives that make up the Heart Sutra, which resonate so strangely and
strongly with the series of apparently anti-Christian negatives that make
up the last chapter of *The Mystical Theology* of Pseudo-Dionysius, are
perfectly reasonable—according to a reason which is beyond reason, of
course.[21]

IMAGES BEYOND IMAGES

But, the deconstruction of images and concepts is not by any means
the end of the matter in either Buddhism or Christianity. The complete
absence of images and concepts is, for Buddhism, the incorrect view of
Nihilism (*ucchedavāda*) and, for Christianity, the denial of the incarnation,
with the result that (for Buddhism) liberation or (for Christianity)
salvation is rendered impossible. Therefore, a means is found to bring
images and concepts back again, but in a subtle and elegant way that
avoids a relapse into the opposite mistakes of Eternalism (*śāśvatavāda*) and
idolatry.

Both Buddhism and Christianity have spiritualities with images
and spiritualities without images. Christianity calls these, respectively,

---

[18] *Mūlamadhyamikakārikā*, 22:1. Quoted in the translation by Kenneth Inada, *Nāgārjuna*
(Tokyo: Hokuseido, 1970), 132.

[19] svabhāvataśca śūnye 'smimścintā naivopapadyate/
param nirodhād bhavati buddho na bhavatīti vā//
—*Mūlamadhyamikakārikā* 22:14. My translation.

[20] na paśyanti tathāgatam: *Mūlamadhyamikakārikā*, 22:15. My translation.

[21] Since these two texts are short, rich, and deserving of close examination and
comparison, they are given in full as an appendix to this article.

cataphatic (sometimes spelled *kataphatic*) and *apophatic*. I have suggested that the appropriate equivalent terms for Buddhism (which, surprisingly, does not seem to have generated them) are *alamkaric* (from the Sanskrit *alaṃkāra*, "ornament") and *apohic* (from the Sanskrit *apoha*, "removing, denying").[22]

It is sometimes argued that the cataphatic/alamkaric spiritualities are preliminary to the apophatic/apohic, and sometimes that these are alternative modes existing in a tension which the traditions do not resolve. I wish to maintain here, however, that there is significant witness in both Buddhism and Christianity to the *coinherence* of the cataphatic/alamkaric and apophatic/apohic modes.

Christianity addressed the issue of the legitimacy or illegitimacy of images in the iconoclastic controversy of the fifth through the seventh centuries.[23] In essence, the main theological aspect of this many-faceted and long drawn-out dispute seems to have been a debate between Platonic and New Testament theisms. Porphyry put the matter bluntly:

> If some Hellenes are light-headed enough to believe that the gods live inside idols, their thought remains much purer than that [of the Christians] who believe that the divinity entered the Virgin Mary's womb, became a foetus, was engendered, and wrapped in clothes, was full of blood, membranes, gall, and even viler things.[24]

Christians who found themselves more or less on the same side as the anti-Christian Porphyry used Biblical passages such as DEUT. 5:7–8 to support their opposition to the presence of images in churches:

> [And God said:] "You will have no gods other than me. You must not make yourselves any image of anything in heaven above or on earth beneath or in the waters under the earth."

The Christians whom we now call Orthodox acknowledged the clarity of these commands, but said that they were not absolute, not binding for all

---

[22] Roger J. Corless, "The Brilliance of Emptiness: T'an-luan as a Mystic of Light", *The Pacific World*, new series, No. 5 (Fall 1989), 13–19.

[23] The western Reformers of the sixteenth and seventeenth centuries revived many of the issues which the iconoclastic controversy had settled, apparently without being aware that they were doing so.

[24] Porphyry, *Against the Christians*, fragment 77. Quoted in *Byzantine Theology: Historical Trends and Doctrinal Themes*, by John Meyendorff (New York: Fordham University Press, second printing of the second edition, with revisions and corrections, 1983), 43.

people at all times and in all places. They were provisional, a function of God's *economy* (*oikonomia*), according to which, in a manner reminiscent of Buddhist *upāya-kauśalya* (skillful means), God adapts his commandments and teaching to his hearers.[25] The Jews, then, says St. John Damascene, needed the prohibition against images "...because of their proneness to idolatry"[26] Christians, however, are more grown up, have a superior revelation and, most importantly, have seen God visibly as Jesus Christ. The commandments against images of God are found in the Old Testament, for God at that time was invisible, but the New Testament calls Jesus the image or icon of the invisible God (*eikōn tou theou aoratou*, COL. 1:15), so that *now*, in the present dispensation, images are allowable:

> In former times God, who is without form or body, could never be depicted. But when God is seen in the flesh conversing with men, I make an image of the God whom I see.[27]

Indeed, it would be heretical *not* to make images of Christ, for if we did not, we would either be maintaining the docetic position that Christ was not genuinely human, or the monophysite position that Christ's human nature was absorbed into his divine nature so that it was invisible or "uncircumscribable".[28] In either case, we would be Platonists, maintaining an ontological distinction between flesh and spirit, not Christians who recognize that, when the Word became flesh, he "deified our flesh for ever, and has sanctified us by surrendering His Godhead to our flesh without confusion."[29]

"Without confusion" is a technical term in Christology, referring to the doctrine of *communicatio idiomatum*, the mutual indwelling, or

---

[25] For an examination of the similarity between economy and skillful means see my article "Lying to Tell the Truth—Upāya in Mahāyāna Buddhism and Oikonomia in Alexandrian Christianity", *Buddha Nature: A Festschrift in Honor of Minoru Kiyota*, edited by Paul J. Griffiths and John P. Keenan (Tokyo: Buddhist Books International, 1990), 27–40.

[26] *First Apology of St. John of Damascus Against Those Who Attack The Divine Images*, 8. Quoted from *St. John of Damascus On the Divine Images,* translated by David Anderson (Crestwood, NY: St. Vladimir's Seminary Press, 1980), 18.

[27] *First Apology*, 16. Quoted in Anderson, 23.

[28] *First Antirrhetic of St. Theodore of Studium*, 2–4. *St. Theodore the Studite On the Holy Icons*, translated by Catharine P. Roth (Crestwood, NY: St. Vladimir's Seminary Press, 1981) 20–23.

[29] John Damascene, *First Apology*, 21. Anderson, 29.

coinherence, of the fullness of the divinity and the fullness of the humanity. If this is so, it follows that:

> The humanity of Christ, which makes the icons possible, is a "new humanity," having been fully restored to communion with God, deified in virtue of the communication of idioms, bearing fully again the image of God. This fact is reflected in iconography as a form of art: the artist thus receives a quasi-sacramental function. Theodore [of Studium] compares the Christian artist to God Himself, making man in His own image: "The fact that God made man in His image and likeness shows that iconography is a divine action." In the beginning God created man in His image. By making an icon of Christ the iconographer also makes an "image of God," for this is what the deified humanity of Jesus truly is.[30]

In Christ, and therefore in the icons, the invisible and the visible coinhere, such that, in the contemplation of icons, the apophatic and cataphatic modes of spirituality are equally present in an image which transcends itself while remaining itself.

Mother Julian of Norwich is a Christian mystic who combines the apophatic and the cataphatic in her spirituality or, to use her terms, the union of bodily and ghostly seeing. Her book, the *Showings* is, at a first reading, entirely cataphatic.

Beginning, as she says, on 13TH. May, 1373, during an illness that seemed as if it might be fatal, but from which she fully recovered, she saw, over a period of days, bright and clear visions of Jesus, Mary, and heaven, and heard detailed commentaries on the visions. The priest had come to give her the last rites, and was holding a crucifix in front of her eyes when, without warning, the crucifix was replaced by the sight of Christ crucified in person:

> And at this, suddenly I saw the red blood running down from under the crown, hot and flowing freely and copiously, a living stream, just as it was at the time when the crown of thorns was pressed on his blessed head. I perceived, truly and powerfully, that it was he who just so, both God and man, himself suffered for me, who showed it to me without any intermediary.[31]

---

[30] Meyendorff, *Byzantine Theology*, 48. The quotation from Theodore is from his *Third Antirrhetic*. See Roth, 101.
[31] Julian of Norwich, *Showings*, translated from the critical text with an introduction by Edmund Colledge O.S.A. and James Walsh S.J. (New York: Paulist Press, 1978), 181.

The blood was so realistic that "...if it had in fact and in substance been happening there, the bed and everything all around it would have been soaked in blood." [32] But, it was simultaneously physical and spiritual, since "...the revelation symbolized and resembled our foul, black mortality, in which our fair, bright, blessed Lord concealed his divinity."[33] The distinctive delight of the Christian life, according to Julian, is the recognition of God's infinite distance and total otherness coinhering with his intense intimacy as a human and as the indwelling life of the soul:

> ...our good Lord, who is so to be revered and feared, is so familiar and so courteous...for truly it is the greatest possible joy, as I see it, that he who is highest and mightiest, noblest and most honourable, is lowest and humblest, most familiar and courteous.[34]

Mother Julian's visions, then, were a true seeing that went beyond seeing yet remained a seeing.

Buddhism concerns itself not so much with the legitimacy or illegitimacy of images[35] as the ontological hardness or softness of conditioned and unconditioned reality, that is, with the presence or absence of inherent existence (*svabhāva*). Having denied that any existence or non-existence has *svabhāva*, that all existence and non-existence is *śūnyatā*, there is the danger that *śūnyatā* will then become the object of misplaced reification. Nāgārjuna warns that any such misplaced reification, such an incorrect grasping (i.e., understanding, *gṛha*) of *śūnyatā* is like grasping a snake by the tail—the snake will bite, and a reified view of *śūnyatā* will block one's progress towards liberation.[36] Understood truly, *śūnyatā* is not a "thing", a statement about what *is*, it is a statement about what is not that leaves space for what is. In a striking medical image, he says:

---

[32] *Showings*, 200.

[33] *Showings*, page 195: "concealed" refers here to the *communicatio idiomatum*. Julian's Middle English has *hyd*. *A Book of Showings to the Anchoress Julian of Norwich*, edited by Edmund Colledge O.S.A. and James Walsh S.J. (Toronto: Pontifical Institute of Mediaeval Studies, 1978) *Studies and Texts*, volume 35, part 2, p. 330.

[34] *Showings*, 188f.

[35] Early Buddhist art did not depict the Buddha anthropomorphically, but it had no hesitation about depicting humans, deities, and so forth. Later, anthropomorphic figures of the Buddha began to be made, and became the norm. The change has not yet been satisfactorily explained, though it seems to have something to do with the rise of the Mahayana.

[36] *Mūlamadhyamakakārikā*, 24:11.

Śūnyata has been proclaimed by the Victorious Ones as the purgative of viewpoints (*dṛṣṭi*). Those for whom *śūnyatā* is a viewpoint are pronounced incurable.[37]

The problem is that *śūnyatā* as "no-thing" may be mis-taken as "nothing"—which, then, would be a "thing". So, at the same time as teaching *śūnyatā* as a "no-thing", Nāgārjuna wants us to realize that it is not separated from "things", from ordinary reality, which is, indeed, the basis on which *śūnyatā* is able to be demonstrated:

> Without relying on conventional reality, the finally established truth cannot be taught, [yet] without going towards the finally established truth, nirvana cannot be obtained.[38]

The two are, finally, coinherent, fully present to each other:

> Nirvana's limit is the limit of samsara. Between the two not even the slightest something may be discerned.[39]

This is the foundation upon which Tantric and Pure Land Buddhism build their practices.[40] Committed to images and visualizations, they do not relinquish them for something supposedly higher and purer, but regard the images themselves as the expression of *śūnyatā*. Thus, the bodies of the visualized entities are symbolically known as rainbow bodies, i.e., like rainbows, they exist, and they exist radiantly, but they do not exist inherently, and the Pure Land Master T'an-luan says that everything in the Pure Land of Amitābha Tathāgata, though visible and apparently physical (and, therefore, apparently defiling) is

---

[37] śūnyatā sarva-dṛṣṭnāṃ proktā niḥsaraṇam jinaiḥ/
yeṣāṃ tu śūnyatā-dṛṣṭis tān asādhyān babhāṣire//
—*Mūlamadhyamakakārikā*, 13:8. My translation.
[38] vyavahāram anāśritya paramārtho na deśyate/
paramārtham anāgamya nirvāṇaṃ nādhigamyate//
—*Mūlamadhyamakakārikā*, 24:10. My translation.
[39] nirvāṇasya ca yā koṭiḥ koṭiḥ saṃsaraṇasya ca/
na tayor-antaraṃ kiṃcit susūkṣmam api vidyate//
—*Mūlamadhyamakakārikā*, 25:20. My translation.
[40] For the similarity between Vajrayāna and Pure Land Buddhism, see my article "Pure Land and Pure Perspective: A Tantric Hermeneutic of Sukhāvatī", *The Pure Land*, new series, No. 6 (December 1989), 205–217.

purifying, since it is the expression of the limitless wisdom and compassion of Amitābha.[41]

Zen Master Dōgen also seems to mean this in the *Kannon*[d] chapter of the *Shōbōgenzō*. In a reference to Case 89 of the Blue Cliff Record,[42] Dōgen comments on a discussion between two past masters about the Bodhisattva Avalokiteśvara in his thousand-armed manifestation.

> Great master Yün-yen Wu-chu asked great master Hsiu-i of Mt. Tao-wu, "How does the Bodhisattva of Great Compassion use his manifold hands and eyes?" Tao-wu replied, "It is like a man reaching behind him in the night searching for a pillow." Yün-yen exclaimed, "I understand, I understand!"[43]

Dōgen says that this answer is not *about* the hands-and-eyes, it itself "...provoked the actual hands and eyes".[44] That is, as a result of the question and answer, Yün-yen's own Avalokiteśvara hands-and-eyes self-manifested. This is the real Avalokiteśvara, not the Avalokiteśvara of the image in the temple, nor the Avalokiteśvara which is the doctrinal hypostasis of great compassion. "It transcends the boundary of even the boundless and unlimited.... This testifies to the fact that although the Tathāgata and Avalokiteśvara manifest their bodies, they are not those particular bodies."[45]

The theme of the teaching is that "There are hands and eyes all over the body",[46] just as it seems to be when one half-consciously fumbles for a pillow that has strayed from one's futon. Or, as the *Cloud of Unknowing* puts it, "...nowhere bodily, is everywhere ghostly."[47]

CONCLUSIONS

I have attempted to demonstrate the polymorphic status of images in Buddhism and Christianity. When images are reified, they are

---

[41] This is repeated like a refrain throughout his *Commentary on the Pure Land Discourse* (*Wang-shêng-lun Chu*[c]) T.40.826–844.

[42] For an English translation of the original case, see Thomas Cleary (trans.), *The Blue Cliff Record* (Boulder, Colo.,: Prajña Press, 1978), 571–577, "The Hands and Eyes of the Bodhisattva of Great Compassion."

[43] *Sounds of Valley Streams: Enlightenment in Dōgen's Zen*, translated by Francis H. Cook (Albany, NY: State University of New York Press, 1989), 89.

[44] Cook, 91.

[45] Cook, 90, 95.

[46] Cook, 89.

[47] *Cloud*, chapter 68. Underhill, 249.

regarded as severe obstacles. According to Buddhism, reification mistakes the fundamental openness and transparency (emptiness, *śūnyatā*) of
reality by filling it with entities having inherent existence (*svabhāva*), thus
blocking the path to liberation. According to Christianity, reification mistakes the true, invisible, uncircumscribed God for a false, visible,
circumscribed idol, which is powerless to save. Buddhism and
Christianity attempt to deconstruct this reification by teaching
spiritualities of negation, in which all images and concepts are discarded.
This deconstruction, however, has its own undesirable consequences. In
Buddhism, it may lead to a belief in nihilism which, if true, would empty
the Dharma of any ability to liberate. In Christianity, even if it does not
lead to outright atheism, it is certainly in danger of denying the validity
of the incarnation and so destroying what Christianity regards as the
only possible means of reconciling creatures and their Creator. Therefore,
the deconstruction of images must itself be deconstructed, that is, it must
in its turn be emptied of misplaced reification. This is done, in
Buddhism, by teaching that reality is the coinherence of samsara and
nirvana and, in Christianity, that in Christ we see the coinherence of
divinity and humanity. This move allows for the presence of images and
concepts which transcend themselves while remaining themselves.

APPENDIX

Two Texts on the Transcendence of Images

A CHRISTIAN APOPHATIC TEXT

THE MYSTICAL THEOLOGY OF PSEUDO-DIONYSIUS:
CHAPTER FIVE

That the supreme Cause of every conceptual thing is not itself conceptual.

Again, as we climb higher we say this. It is not soul or mind, nor does it possess imagination, conviction, speech, or understanding. Nor is it speech per se, understanding per se. It cannot be spoken of and it cannot be grasped by understanding. It is not number or order, greatness or smallness, equality or inequality, similarity or dissimilarity. It is not immovable, moving, or at rest. It has no power, it is not power, nor is it light. It does not live nor is it life. It is not a substance, nor is it eternity or time. It cannot be grasped by the understanding since it is neither knowledge nor truth. It is not kingship. It is not wisdom. It is neither one nor oneness, divinity nor goodness. Nor is it a spirit, in the sense in which we understand that term. It is not sonship or fatherhood and it is nothing known to us or to any other being. It falls neither within the predicate of nonbeing nor of being. Existing beings do not know it as it actually is and it does not know them as they are. There is no speaking of it, nor name nor knowledge of it. Darkness and light, error and truth—it is none of these. It is beyond assertion and denial. We make assertions and denials of what is next to it but never of it, for it is both beyond every assertion, being the perfect and unique cause of all things, and, by virtue of its preeminently simple and absolute nature, free of every limitation, beyond every limitation; it is also beyond every denial.

Pseudo-Dionysius: The Complete Works,
translated by Colm Luibheid
(New York: Paulist Press, 1987), page 141

A BUDDHIST APOHIC TEXT

THE SUTRA ON THE HEART OF THE TRANSCENDENT AND VICTORIOUS PERFECTION OF WISDOM

Thus did I hear at one time. The Transcendent Victor was sitting on Vulture Mountain in Rājagṛha together with a great assembly of monks and a great assembly of Bodhisattvas. At that time the Transcendent Victor was absorbed in a samādhi on the enumerations of phenomena called "perception of the profound." Also at that time, the Bodhisattva, the Mahāsattva, the Superior Avalokiteśvara was contemplating the meaning of the profound perfection of wisdom and he saw that those five aggregates also are empty of inherent existence. Then, by the power of the Buddha, the venerable Śāriputra said this to the Bodhisattva, the Mahāsattva, the Superior Avalokiteśvara, "How should a son of good lineage train who wishes to practice the profound perfection of wisdom?"

The Bodhisattva, the Mahāsattva, the Superior Avalokiteśvara said this to the venerable Śāriputra: "Śāriputra, a son of good lineage or a daughter of good lineage who wishes to practice the profound perfection of wisdom should view [things] in this way: They should correctly view those five aggregates also as empty of inherent existence. Form is emptiness; emptiness is form. Emptiness is not other than form; form is not other than emptiness. In the same way, feeling, discrimination, compositional factors, and consciousnesses are empty. Śāriputra, in that way, all phenomena are empty, that is, without characteristic, unproduced, unceased, stainless, not stainless, undiminished, unfilled. Therefore, Śāriputra, in emptiness, there is no form, no feeling, no discrimination, no compositional factors, no consciousness, no eye, no ear, no nose, no tongue, no body, no mind, no form, no sound, no odor, no taste, no object of touch, no phenomenon. There is no eye constituent, no mental constituent, up to and including no mental consciousness constituent. There is no ignorance, no extinction of ignorance, up to and including no aging and death and no extinction of aging and death. Similarly, there are no sufferings, no origins, no cessations, no paths, no exalted wisdom, no attainment, and also no non-attainment.

Therefore, Śāriputra, because Bodhisattvas have no attainment, they depend on and abide in the perfection of wisdom; because their minds are without obstructions, they are without fear. Having completely passed beyond all error they go to the completion of nirvāṇa. All the Buddhas who abide in the three times have been fully awakened into unsurpassed, perfect, complete enlightenment through relying on the perfection of wisdom.

Therefore, the mantra of the perfection of wisdom is the mantra of great knowledge, the unsurpassed mantra, the mantra equal to the unequalled, the mantra that thoroughly pacifies all suffering. Because it is not false, it should be known to be true. The mantra of the perfection of wisdom is stated:

tadyatha oṃ gate gate paragate parasaṃgate bodhi svaha

Śāriputra, Bodhisattva Mahāsattvas should train in the profound perfection of wisdom in that way."

Then the Transcendent Victor rose from that samādhi and said to the Bodhisattva, the Mahāsattva, the Superior Avalokiteśvara, "Well done. Well done, well done, child of good lineage, it is just so. Child of good lineage, it is like that; the profound perfection of wisdom should be practiced just as you have taught it. Even the Tathāgatas admire this." The Transcendent Victor having so spoken, the venerable Śāriputra, the Bodhisattva, the Mahāsattva, the Superior Avalokiteśvara, and all those surrounding and those of the world, the gods, humans, demigods, and *gandharvas* were filled with admiration and praised the words of the Transcendent Victor.

Translated from the Tibetan version by
Donald S. Lopez, Jr., *The Heart Sūtra Explained*
(Albany, NY: State University of New York Press, 1988),
pages 19–20

CHINESE CHARACTER INDEX

a   佛向上事

b   非佛

c   往生論註

d   觀音

Dead Words, Living Words, and Healing Words

THE DISSEMINATIONS OF DŌGEN AND ECKHART

DAVID LOY
BUNKYO UNIVERSITY

What does Derrida's type of deconstruction imply about religion and for religion? Recently this issue has become more important to Derrida and some of those influenced by his work.[1] In his most protracted discussion to date on the relationship between deconstruction and religion, *"Comment ne pas parler: Dénégations"* (translated as "How to Avoid Speaking: Denials"), Derrida has been primarily concerned to distinguish deconstruction from negative theology. The apophatic language of negative theology suggests a project similar to his, yet the uses to which that language is put have been quite different. Negative theologies tend to conclude that, since all predicative language is inadequate to express the nature of God, only a negative attribution can approach him; this denies God any attributable essence, but merely to reserve a hyperessentiality, a being beyond Being. Derrida refers specifically to Eckhart and we can see his point in Eckhart's great sermon on the text "Blessed are the poor...", where Eckhart declares: "Therefore I pray God that he may rid me of God, for unconditioned being is above God and all distinctions." That we can refer to any such unconditioned being is incompatible with Derrida's argument that there is no

---

[1] See, for example, Harold Coward and Toby Foshay, eds., *Derrida and Negative Theology* (Albany: State University of New York, 1992). This includes two essays by Derrida: "Of an Apocalyptic Tone Recently Adopted in Philosophy" and "How to Avoid Speaking: Denials"; Christian, Buddhist and Hindu reactions to those essays; and responses by Derrida.

"transcendental signified", since every process of signification, including all supposed self-presence, is an economy of differences. "There are only, everywhere, differences and traces of differences."[2]

Even if this particular point is accepted, however, a great deal remains to be said on the issue and, needless to say, we are not limited to considering Derrida's own views. One place to start—or rather (since we never begin at the beginning) one textual strand I would like to continue spinning—is a fine paper by John D. Caputo titled "Mysticism and Transgression: Derrida and Meister Eckhart".[3] In this essay Caputo is concerned that Derrida's deconstruction has been too easily tied with the familiar death-of-God scenario and used to refute the possibility of God or the sacred. Criticizing this as reductionist, Caputo argues for what he calls the "armed neutrality" of Derrida's *différance*: *armed* because it holds all existence claims suspect, yet ontologically *neutral* because it does not imply the existence or non-existence of any entity. *Différance* establishes the possibility of a language that addresses God just as much as a discourse that denies God, for it does not settle the God-question one way or another. "In fact, it *un*settles it, by showing that any debate about the existence of God is beset by the difficulties which typically inhabit such debates, by their inevitable recourse to binary pairs which cannot be made to stick" (p. 28).

It is easy to see why deconstructionists might be uncomfortable with this conclusion, inasmuch as the God-quest has usually been our search for an Unconditioned which grounds us. Nonetheless, I think Caputo is correct, and perhaps more so than he realizes. It may be easier to see this if we shift from God-talk to Buddha-talk, for the point I want to make has been expressed more clearly in the Buddhist tradition. Buddhism, like many other Asian traditions, does not accept the distinction that the West has come to make between religion and philosophy, which is why what needs to be *un*settled in Mahayāna is neither the God-question nor the Buddha-question but most of all the "commonsense" everyday world, riddled as it is with unconscious, because automatized, ontological committments. Mādhyamika can argue that the limits [*koti*] of

---

[2] Jacques Derrida, *Positions,* trans. Alan Bass (University of Chicago Press, 1981), 26. The Buddhist doctrine of *pratītya-samutpāda* makes the same point about consciousness.

[3] "Mysticism and Transgression: Derrida and Meister Eckhart" in *Derrida and Deconstruction,* ed. Hugh J. Silverman (Routledge: New York and London, 1989), 24–39.

this world are the same as the limits of *nirvāṇa*[4] because our everyday world has been mentally-conditioned and socially-constructed by our delusive attribution of self-existence to objects. So we experience the world as a collection of discrete, self-existing things which interact causally *in* objective space and time; and that leads to suffering insofar as we understand ourselves too to be such self-existing things, who are nonetheless subject to the ravages of time and change—who are born only to become ill, grow old, and die.

This implies a more radical possibility for the *un*settling that Caputo refers to and that *différance* certainly implies: for merely by subverting such ontological claims, and without making any metaphysical claims of its own, the Buddhist deconstruction of all such self-existence (especially our own) can allow something else to shine forth—something that has always been there/here yet has been overlooked in our haste to objectify things in order to fixate on them. Such deconstruction can heal us by revealing a less dualistic way not only of understanding but of experiencing the relation between ourselves and the supposedly objective world.

For Buddhism this sense of separation between me and the world lies at the heart of our *duḥkha*, i.e., of our notorious inability to be happy. Buddhism relates our dis-ease to the delusive nature of the ego-self, which like everything else is a manifestation of the universe *yet feels separate from it*. The basic difficulty is that insofar as "I" feel separate (i.e., an autonomous, self-existing consciousness) I also feel uncomfortable, because an *illusory* sense of separateness will inevitably be insecure. The unavoidable trace of nothingness in my fictitious (because not really self-existing) sense-of-self is therefore experienced as a sense-of-lack; and in reaction the sense-of-self becomes preoccupied with trying to make itself—it's-self—self-existing, in one or another symbolic fashion. The tragic irony is that the ways we attempt to do this cannot succeed, for a sense-of-self can never expel the trace of lack that always shadows it insofar as it is illusory; while in the most important sense we are already self-existing, since *the infinite set of differential traces that constitutes each of us is nothing less than the whole universe.* "The self-existence of a Buddha is the self-existence of this very cosmos. The Buddha is without a self-existent nature; the cosmos too is without a self-existent nature."[5] What Nāgārjuna says here about the Buddha is equally true for each of us, and

---

[4] *Mūlamadhyamikakārikā* 24: 19.
[5] *Mūlamadhyamikakārikā* 24: 16.

for that matter everything in the universe; the difference is that a Buddha (and a Christ?) knows it. I think this touches on the enduring attraction of what Heidegger calls onto-theology and what Derrida calls logocentrism, not just in the West but everywhere: Being/being means security to us because it means a ground for the self, whether that is understood as experiencing Transcendence or intellectually sublimated into a metaphysical principle underlying everything. We want to meet God face-to-face, or gain enlightenment, but the fact that everything is *śūnya* means we can never attain them. We can, however, realize what we have always been/not been.[6]

In accordance with this, Mādhyamika and Ch'an Buddhism have no teaching to transmit, no doctrine that must be believed in order to be a Buddhist, or that must be grasped in order to be saved. If our ways of living in the world are what need to be unsettled, what is to be taught will vary according to the person and the situation, because people fixate on different things. "If I tell you that I have a system of *dharma* [teaching] to transmit to others, I am cheating you," declared the sixth Ch'an patriarch Hui-neng. "What I do to my disciples is to liberate them from their own bondage with such devices as the case may need."[7]

This type of unsettling does not leave the God-question or the Buddha-question in abeyance: it resolves it—not, however, by giving us an answer to those questions in the place we look for it, but by providing a different way of experiencing, by deconstructing our everyday world into a different one. At the same time (and this reappropriates Caputo's point) it must also be said that from another perspective this nondual way of experiencing nonetheless deepens the religious question, because it still leaves the world *essentially* mysterious in a fashion that cannot be resolved but does not need to be resolved: every nondual "thing" or

---

[6] The self-existence (Sanskrit, *sva-bhāva*) that Mādhyamika refutes corresponds to the "self-presence" which Derrida criticizes in textual terms, by showing that every process of signification, including self-consciousness, is an economy of differences. Self-presence "has never been given but only dreamed of and always already split, incapable of appearing to itself except in its own disapperance." Discussions of this argument tend to focus on the *-presence* of self-presence, but the *self-* needs to be emphasized as much. It is "the hunger for/of self" that seeks fulfillment in "the absolute phantasm" of "absolute self-having." (*Of Grammatology*, 112; "an Apocalyptic Tone', 90, 91) For more on the sense-of-lack as "shadow" of the sense-of-self, see David Loy, *Lack and Transcendence,* (Atlantic Highlands, New Jersey: Humanities Press, 1996).
[7] *The Diamond Sutra and the Sutra of Hui Neng,* tran. A. F. Price and Wong Moulam (Boston: Shambhala, 1990), 132.

event acquires a numinous quality which cannot be fully understood causally or reductively.

What does this Buddhist deconstruction imply about language? How does it affect the ways we hear and speak, read and write? There is some support in the Buddhist tradition, as in negative theology generally, for denying or at least depreciating the value of language. The implication is that linguistic meaning is so inevitably dualistic that it can never adequately describe or express reality; therefore a wise person speaks seldom and little. Nāgārjuna denied that he had any views of his own: "If I had a position, no doubt fault could be found with it. Since I have no position, that problem does not arise." How could he avoid taking a position? "Ultimate serenity is the coming to rest of all ways of taking things, the repose of named things; no truth has been taught by a Buddha for anyone, anywhere."[8] This "coming to rest of all ways of taking things" is also found in Ch'an—for example, in the way that Tung-shan Shou-ch'u (d. 990) distinguished between dead words and living words: "If there is any rational intention manifested in the words, then they are dead words; if there is no rational intention manifested in the words, then they are living words."[9] Tung-shan does not deny the usefulness of language but does question its "rational" function—which seems to mean, he denies its validity as a way to understand or "take" things. More recently, the Japanese Zen scholar and popularizer D. T. Suzuki has perpetuated a similar distinction in the way he explains the process of working on a *kōan*: the purpose of a *kōan* is to subvert all rational attempts to solve it, he claimed, whereupon we may be transported into a different and nonrational way of experiencing it and the world, including language.

There is a problem with this understanding of "enlightened language", and it is a mistake to conclude that Tung-shan's or Suzuki's view is *the* Buddhist or *the* Mahāyāna view of language (even if we ignore the obvious contradiction that would seem to involve!). The difficulty with denigrating "rational intentions" and trying to "end all ways of taking things" is that this tends to reinforce the deluded dualism we already make between words and things, between thought and world. The danger is that we will "take" language/thought as a filter that should be eliminated in order to experience things/the world more

---

[8] *Vigraha-vyāvartanī* 29; *Mūlamadhamikakārikā* 25:24.
[9] In Chang Chung-yuan, *Original Teachings of Ch'an Buddhism* (New York: Vintage, 1971), 271.

immediately—an approach which unfortunately reconstitutes the problem of dualism in the means chosen to overcome it. An alternative approach was hinted at by Ch'an master Yün-men Wen-yen (d. 949): "There are words which go beyond words. This is like eating rice everyday without any attachment to a grain of rice."[10] Hui-neng tells us how words can go beyond words, in the process of explaining why he has no *dharma* to transmit to others:

> Only those who do not possess a single system of *dharma* can formulate all systems of *dharma* , and only those who can understand the meaning [of this paradox] may use such terms. It makes no difference to those who have realized the essence of mind whether they formulate all systems of *dharma* or dispense with all of them. They are at liberty to come or to go. They are free from obstacles or impediments. They take appropriate actions as circumstances require. They give suitable answers according to the temperament of the inquirer.[11]

For Caputo, following Derrida, Eckhart's "godhead beyond god" is another signifer with transcendental pretensions (p. 33), which needs to be deconstructed and shown to be the function of a network of differences (a deconstruction that, for example, Nāgārjuna performs on *nirvāṇa* in chapter 25 of the *Mūlamadhyamikakārikā*). For Derrida no words go beyond words, yet these words of the sixth patriarch imply that for Buddhism there is another perspective where one signifier does not necessarily equal another or simply reduce to being a function of others. I think there is no better way to gain an appreciation of how words can go beyond words than by considering how Hui-neng, Dōgen and Eckhart understood language. And the best way to understand their understanding of language is, of course, to look at how they actually used words.

II

Hui-neng, Dōgen and Eckhart: arguably the greatest Chinese Ch'an master, the greatest Japanese Zen master, and the greatest medieval Christian mystical writer. They are so elevated in our pantheon of religious heroes that we are apt to overlook how opportunistic—indeed,

---

[10] *Original Teachings of Ch'an Buddhism*, 271.
[11] *The Sutra of Hui Neng*, 132.

how completely *unscrupulous*—they were in the ways they employed language. [12]

Hui-neng's opportunism is obvious in the two passages from his *Platform Sutra* already quoted above. His own words provide some excellent instances of language "free from obstacles or impediments", of teachings that "give suitable answers according to the temperament of the inquirer." To cite only one example, in one place the sixth patriarch does not hesitate to contradict received Buddhist teachings, in response to the question of a monk, Chang Hsing-ch'ang, who could not understand the meaning of the terms "eternal" and "not eternal" in the *Mahaparinirvana Sutra.*

> "What is not eternal is the buddha-nature," replied the patriarch, "and what is eternal is the discriminating mind together with all meritorious and demeritorious dharmas."
> "Your explanation, sir, contradicts the sutra," said Chang.
> "I dare not, since I inherit the heart seal of Lord Buddha.... If buddha-nature is eternal, it would be of no use to talk about meritorious and demeritorious dharmas; and until the end of a *kalpa* no one would arouse the *bodhicitta*. Therefore, *when I say 'not eternal' it is exactly what Lord Buddha meant for 'eternal.'* Again, if all dharmas are not eternal, then every thing or object would have a nature of its own [i.e., self-existence or essence] to suffer death and birth. In that case, it would mean that the essence of mind, which is truly eternal, does not pervade everywhere. *Therefore when I say 'eternal' it is exactly what Lord Buddha meant by 'not eternal.'.* . . In following slavishly the wording of the sutra, you have ignored the spirit of the text."

From this passage alone it is difficult to understand why Hui-neng reversed the meaning of the two terms; we would need to know more about the situation within which this dialogue took place, the con-text of the text. But apparently it worked: "All of a sudden Chang awoke to full enlightenment." Whether we find Hui-neng's explanation helpful or not, the most important point here is that, by his own criterion, there is no arguing with such success.

In his final instructions to his successors before passing away, Hui-neng taught more about how to teach: " Whenever a man puts a question to you, answer him in antonyms, so that a pair of opposites will be formed, such as coming and going. When the interdependence of the two

---

[12] Scruple is from the Latin *scrupulus,* itself derived from *scrupus* a rough or hard pebble, used figuratively by Cicero for a cause of uneasiness or anxiety. The Latin *opportun-us* means fit, suitable, convenient, seasonable; advantageous, serviceable.

is entirely done away with there would be, in the absolute sense, neither coming nor going."[13] If someone is fixated on one view, challenge him with the opposite view—not to convert him to that view but to unsettle him from all views, so that one might slip out between them.

> Language and symbols circumscribe; but, as living forces, they are dynamic enough to open up, constantly re-expressing, renewing, and casting-off, so as to unfold new horizons of their own life. In this way language and symbols know no limits with respect to how far they can penetrate both conceptually and symbolically. No Buddhist thinker was more intensely and meticulously involved with the exploration of each and every linguistic possibility of Buddhist concepts and symbols—even those forgotten, displaced ones—than Dōgen who endeavored to appropriate them in the dynamic workings of the Way's realization. (Hee-jin Kim)[14]

Many Buddhists believe that concepts are inherently delusive, that they should be eliminated in order to realize our true nature. **Dōgen's** approach was the complete opposite, and he devoted much energy to demonstrating the importance of language and its possibilities. Before discussing his understanding of language, however, we must notice how he used it.

> Throughout the *Shōbōgenzō*, Dōgen painstakingly dissects a given passage and explores its semantic possibilities at every turn, literally turning the conventional diction upside down and inside out. The result is a dramatic shift in our perception and understanding of the original passage. One of the most rewarding aspects of translating Dōgen's *Shōbōgenzō* is his radical challenge to ordinary language. *To Dōgen the manner of expression is as important as the substance of thought; in fact, the experimentation with language is equivalent to the making of reality.* Furthermore, Dōgen frequently puts forth deliberate, often brilliant, "misinterpretations" of certain notions and passages of Buddhism. This distortion of original meaning is not due to any ignorance of Chinese or Japanese (indeed, it testifies to a unique mastery of both) but rather to a different kind of thinking—the logic of the Buddha-dharma. (Kim)[15]

---

[13] *The Sutra of Hui Neng*, 134–135, 142. My italics.

[14] Hee-jin Kim, "Method and Realization: Dōgen's Use of the Kōan Language", 9, presented at a conference on "The Significance of Dōgen", Tassajara Zen Mountain Center, October 8–11, 1981.

[15] Hee-jin Kim, "The Reason of Words and Letters": Dōgen and Kōan Language", in William R. LaFleur, ed., *Dōgen Studies* (Honolulu: University of Hawaii, 1985), 60. My italics.

Among the many examples which may be cited, here are some of the most interesting:

Dōgen's discussion of *tō-higan* ("reaching the other shore") transposes the two characters into *higan-tō*, "the other shore's arrival" or "the other shore has arrived." The transcribed term no longer refers to a future event but emphasizes the event of realization here and now.

Seppō "preaching the dharma" is reversed in the same way to become *hō-setsu* "the dharma's preaching." This allows Dōgen to say: "This 'discourse on the Dharma' is 'the Dharma's discourse.'"

Dōgen takes the term *arutoki* ("at a certain time, sometimes, once") and recombines its components *u* "to be, to have" and *ji* "time, occasion" to make *uji*, "being-time", which he uses to signify the nonduality of existence and time.

Perhaps the best known example of this particular technique is in the *Busshō* fascicle, which quotes from the *Nirvana Sutra*: "All sentient beings without exception have Buddha-nature". Dōgen rearranges the syntactical components to make them mean: All sentient beings, i.e., all existence, *is* Buddha-nature. As Kim points out, this changes potentiality into actuality, and it liberates us from anthropocentrism. Sentient beings, everything that exists and Buddha-nature all become nondual.

Like Heidegger, Dōgen converts nouns into verbs and uses them to predicate the same noun, in order to say, e.g., "the sky skys the sky." This allows him to escape the subject-predicate dualism of language and point out that, for example, spring "passes without anything outside itself."

The *Zazenshin* fascicle of the *Shōbōgenzō* reinterprets a *kōan* about thinking (*shiryō*), not-thinking (*fu-shiryō*), and non-thinking (*hi-shiryō*). The original *kōan*, which Dōgen quotes, reads as follows:

> After sitting, a monk asked Great Master Yueh-shan Hung-tao: "What are you thinking in the immobile state of sitting?" The master answered: "I think of not-thinking." The monk asked: "How can one think of not-thinking?" The master said: "Nonthinking."

Dōgen transforms Yueh-shan's "I think of not-thinking" into "Thinking is not-thinking." *Fu-shiryō* becomes *fu no shiryō*: the not's, or (as Kim puts it) the absolute emptiness's, thinking. That is, *fu-shiryō* no longer refers to the absence or denial of thinking, but suggests instead that authentic thinking is "the not's thinking".

What ties together all these remarkable examples is more than that Dōgen unscrupulously twists traditional texts to make them mean whatever he wants them to say. In each case Dōgen is conflating a problematic dualism, that is, a deluded way of thinking which causes problems for us. *Higan-tō* denies the usual duality between practice and realization. *Hō-setsu* denies any duality between the one who preaches the *dharma* and the *dharma* that is taught. The *Busshō* fascicle denies the duality between sentient beings and their Buddha-nature. *Uji* denies any duality between beings and their temporality; converting nouns into verbs allows Dōgen to deny, e.g., the duality between springtime and things *in* springtime. *Fu no shiryō* denies the especially dangerous dualism (for Buddhist practitioners) between thinking and not-thinking (as it occurs in *zazen*); practice is not a matter of getting rid of thinking but realizing the "emptiness" of thinking. *In each instance Dōgen does not allow himself to be limited by the usual dualisms of our language, and of our thought, but concocts expressions that leap out of the bifurcations we get stuck in.* For Kim it is "abundantly clear that in these linguistic and symbolic transformations Dōgen acts as a magician or an alchemist of language conjuring up an infinity of symbolic universes freely and selflessly as the self-expressions of Buddha-nature."[16]

One more type of conflation (or deconstruction) should be noticed before we attempt to characterize this way of using language. In Buddhism a number of metaphors have become traditional as ways to contrast this world of suffering with the realm of enlightenment: for example, *gabyō* (pictured cakes, which cannot satisfy us when we are hungry), *kūge* (literally sky-flowers, seen when the eye is defective, hence a metaphor for illusory perceptions), *kattō* (entangling vines, meaning worldly attachments), and *mu* (a dream, as opposed to being awake). Dōgen elevates all these depreciated terms by revitalizing them. Instead of dismissing pictures (i.e., concepts), he emphasizes their importance: "Because the entire world and all dharmas are unequivocally pictures, men and dharmas are actualized through pictures, and the buddhas and patriarchs are perfected through pictures." *Kūge*, usually castigated as illusions, he revalorizes as "flowers of emptiness"; in place of the typical Buddhist duality between reality and delusion, "all dharmas of the universe are the flowers of emptiness." Instead of the usual admonition to cut off all entangling vines, Dōgen emphasizes the importance of worldly relationships. And "all dharmas in the dream state as well as in the waking state are equally ultimate reality.... Dream and waking are

---

[16] "The Reason of Words and Letters", 63.

equally ultimate reality: no largeness or smallness, no superiority or inferiority has anything to do with them."[17]

These last examples, in particular, leave us no doubt about Dōgen's understanding of language. Concepts, metaphors, parables and so forth are not just instrumental, convenient means to communicate truth, for they themselves manifest the truth—or rather, since that way of putting it is still too dualistic, they themselves are the truth that we need to realize.

> Words are no longer just something that the intellect manipulates abstractly and impersonally but something that works intimately in the existential metabolism of one who uses them philosophically and religiously in a special manner and with a special attitude. They are no longer mere means or symbols that point to realities other than themselves but are themselves the realities of original enlightenment and the Buddha-nature. (Kim) [18]

"Metaphor in Dōgen's sense is not that which points to something other than itself, but that in which something realizes itself", summarizes Kim. "In short, the symbol is not a means to edification but an end in itself—the workings of ultimate truth." As Dōgen himself puts it: "The Buddha-dharma, even if it is a metaphor, is ultimate reality."[19] If the metaphor is not used to compensate for my own lack of self-existence— which makes me try to get some graspable truth *from* it—it can be a way my mind consummates itself: although symbols can be redeemed only by mind, the mind does not function in a vacuum but is activated by symbols.

In the *Sansuikyō* fascicle of the *Shōbōgenzō* Dōgen criticizes those who have an instrumentalist view of language: "How pitiable are they who are unaware that discriminating thought *is* words and phrases, and that words and phrases *liberate* discriminating thought." Kim provides a valuable gloss on this memorable phrase: "In spite of inherent frailties in their make-up, words are the bearer of ultimate truth. In this respect, words are not different from things, events, or beings—all 'alive' in Dōgen's thought."[20]

Alive, because language, like any other thing or event, is (and must be realized to be) *ippō-gūjin*, "the total exertion of a single dharma." This

---

[17] "The Reason of Words and Letters", 66 ff.
[18] Hee-Jin Kim, *Dōgen Kigen—Mystical Realist* (Tucson: University of Arizona Press, 1975), 110. When was the last time your Zen master told you *that*?
[19] In the *Muchū-setsumu* fascicle, as quoted in "The Reason of Words and Letters", 73.
[20] "The Reason of Words and Letters", 57, 58.

term, a key one for Dōgen, embodies his dynamic understanding of the Hua-yen doctrine of interpenetration. According to Hua-yen, each *dharma* (here meaning any thing or event, and for Dōgen this explicitly includes linguistic expressions) is both the cause of and the effect of all other *dharmas* in the universe. This interfusion means that the life of one *dharma* becomes the life of all *dharmas*, as there is nothing but that *dharma* in the whole universe. Since no *dharma* interferes with any other *dharma* —because each is nothing other than an expression of all the others— *dharmas* transcend all dualism; in this way they are both harmonious with all other dharmas yet function as if independent of them.[21]

If we apply this Hua-yen view of *dharmas* to language, words and metaphors can be understood not just as instrumentally trying to grasp and convey truth (and thereby dualistically interfering with our realization of some truth that transcends words) but as being the truth— that is, as one of the many ways that Buddha-nature *is*. A birdsong, a temple bell ringing, a flower blooming, and Dōgen's words too blooming for us as we read or hear them... if we do not dualize between world and word (and Dōgen shows us we do not need to dualize between them), then we can experience the Buddha-dharma—our own "empty" nature—presencing (but not *self*-presencing: each manifests the whole universe) and playing in each.

Dōgen is more literary than Hui-neng, yet I do not see any fundamental difference in their teachings and in their views of language. Like Beethoven and the Romantic tradition that followed him, Hui-neng forged a path that others explored more fully, in this case by developing the Ch'an tradition.... Is there anyone comparable to Hui-neng and Dōgen in Christianity?

> He is a master of life *and* a master of the letter who plays with the syntax and semantics of the scriptural texts and the texts of the masters before him in order to tease out of them ever new senses. He is a master of repetition who knew well that his commentary was not to be a simple reproduction

---

[21] This apparent paradox is a crucial point, yet explaining it and defending it would shift the focus of this essay. It may be understood as the Chinese version of Nāgārjuna's argument in the *Mūlamadhyamikakārikā*, which uses causality to refute the self-existence of anything, and then denies causal relationships: "That which, taken as causal or dependent, is the process of being born and passing on, is, taken non-causally and beyond all dependence, declared to be *nirvāṇa*." (25: 19) For more on this, see my *Nonduality: A Study in Comparative Philosophy* (Yale, 1988) chapter 6, and "The Deconstruction of Buddhism" in *Derrida and Negative Theology* (cited in fn 1).

but a new production, a new rendering which made the old text speak anew and say what had not been heard. He was constantly altering the syntax of a text, rewriting it so that it said something new. He would fuss with trivial features of a text to which no attention at all had been paid and make everything turn on them, even to the point of reversing their traditional meaning.... He would invert sayings to see what fruit they would yield.

Is this more of Kim on Dōgen? It could be, but in fact it's Caputo on Eckhart. Let us let him finish his point.

There is no better example, to my knowledge, of a certain mystical dissemination and a religiously joyful wisdom than the brilliantly, playful virtuosity of Eckhart's German sermons and Latin treatises. He rewrites the words of Scripture, turns and twists the most familiar sacred stories, reinterprets the oldest teachings in the most innovative and shocking ways.... And always with the same effect: to prod the life of the spirit, to promote its vitality, to raise its pitch, to enhance its energy. Like a religious answer to Nietzsche six centuries before the fact, Eckhart engages with Dionysian productivity in a multiplication of religious fictions which serve the interests of a "life" which lives out of its own superabundance, without why or wherefore, for the sake of life itself... [22]

"There is a grammatological exuberance, a transgressive energy, in Eckhart", summarizes Caputo, and because of his own exuberance we can readily forgive the trendy vocabulary (today everyone seems rather too eager to transgress!). However, we need some examples.

Eckhart reads *mutuo* (reciprocal) as *meo tuo et tuo meo* (mine yours and yours mine). He plays with the name of his own religious order (*ordo praedicatorum*, order of preachers) to make it an "order of praisers", i.e., those who offer divine predicates. In the Vulgate version of Romans 6:22, *Nun vero liberati a peccato* ("Now, however, you have been liberated from sin'"), Eckhart discovers eight different grammatical functions in *vero*, including: truly (*vere*) delivered from sin; delivered from sin by truth (*vero*, the datum of *verum*), and so forth. At the beginning of the Gospel of John, *In principio erat verbum*, the words *principium*, *erat* and *verbum* are submitted to similar readings, multiplying and disseminating their meanings. Perhaps the most shocking of all, Eckhart presumes to change the opening lines of the *Pater Noster* (believed to be the only prayer we have from Jesus) so that "thy will be done" becomes '"will, be thine [i.e.,

---

[22] "Mysticism and Transgression," 35.

God's]", because he believed that willing to do God's will is not as good as getting beyond willing altogether.[23]

In the famous story where Jesus said that Mary had chosen the better part (the *vita contemplativa*), Eckhart reverses the traditional understanding by explaining that the repetition of Martha's name ("Martha, Martha, you worry and fret about so many things") means that she had two gifts, the *vita activa* as well as the *vita contemplativa*, and therefore Martha had chosen the better part! This follows from Eckhart's emphasis on spiritual vitality, his teaching that true thankfulness is fruitfulness (i.e., to be made fruitful by the gift one receives, to give birth from it in return). Caputo concludes his article by praising this typical "mystical perversity" whereby Eckhart argues that the better part belongs not to Mary "languishing dreamily at the feet of Jesus, trying to be one with the One" but to Martha who rushes here and there preparing for Jesus' visit "with all the energy and robustness of life."

Perhaps the most significant instance of Eckhart's unscrupulous use of language is the way he plays with the binary terms Being and Nonbeing (or Nothing) by nonchalantly reversing their meaning. Sometimes he refers to the being of creatures and describes God as a nothing, without the slightest bit of existence. At other times he contrasts the "nullity" of all creatures with the being of God, in which case it is not that God has being, or even that God is being, but that being is God (*esse est deus*). Caputo says that Eckhart "understands quite well that the terms 'Being' and 'Nothing' are functions of each other, that each is inscribed in the other, marked and traced by the other, and that neither gets the job done, alone or together" (p. 31). Well put, yet Eckhart, like Dōgen, plays with syntax and semantics not just to tease out ever new senses, not just to see how many meanings he can make dance on the head of a pin, but to develop some special types of expression, particularly those which can help us to see through the duality between ourselves and God. In the *Busshō* fascicle Dōgen reorders syntax to make "All beings have Buddha-nature" into "All beings are Buddha-nature"; Eckhart is happy to reverse the referents of Being and Nothingness to the same end, without ever asserting that both God *and* creatures have being, for that would involve a dualism between the two: if God is nothing it is because he is *our* nothingness, and if we are nothing it is because all our being is actually God's. The same denial of that same duality occurs in reading "thy will

---

[23] "Mysticism and Transgression," 37. Caputo refers to Frank Tobin's study *Meister Eckhart: Thought and Language* (Philadelphia: University of Pennsylvania Press, 1986), 171–179.

be done" as "will, be thine [God's]". And Eckhart uses the story of Mary and Martha to deny a derivative dualism between the contemplative life and the active life.

Caputo does not deny a more orthodox side to Eckhart, which denies God (*Deus*) the better to assert the Godhead (*Deitas*) and which understands that Godhead as a super-essentiality more real than reality. That is one tendency in Eckhart's writings, yet it is not the only aspect or for us the most significant aspect. "'I pray God that he may make me free of God' is an ongoing prayer which keeps the discourse open. This is a prayer against closure, against turning the latest and best creations of discourse into idols. It arises from an ongoing distrust of our ineradicable desire for presence, of our insidious tendency to arrest the play and build an altar to a produced effect" (p. 34). This is so well-expressed that I hesitate to quibble; yet, again, I think that Eckhart is concerned with more than resisting conceptual closure. Although he doesn't want to build altars to the products of his originality, his linguistic play is happy to produce them because he wants to do something more than keep the conversation going. Like Hui-neng and Dōgen, he wants us to change the ways we experience and live "in" the world.

That brings us to a crucial question which can no longer be avoided. If, as I have been trying to show, Hui-neng, Dōgen and Eckhart exemplify a freedom with language that Derrida has more recently celebrated; if their writings contain some of the best examples of the liberated kind of dissemination that Derrida's deconstruction implies, which is not pious of any produced effects but is ready to challenge them all; then what is the difference, if any, between what Derrida is doing and what they are doing? What makes their deconstructive disseminations "religious" and Derrida's not?

III

The answer to this question is most evident in Dōgen, although a similar response is implicit in Hui-neng's and Eckhart's writings.

Earlier, in a discussion of *ippō-gūjin* ("the total exertion of a single *dharma*") aspect of language, it was emphasized that language for Dōgen does not just instrumentally attempt to grasp and convey truth, it *is* truth: that is, one of the ways that Buddhanature *is*. But of course that is not to deny that language is instrumental as well. The point of the Hua-

yen doctrine of interpenetration is that each *dharma* is both the cause and
the effect of all other *dharmas*. One way to understand this is that
linguistic expressions are at the same time both means—they refer to
other things—and ends in themselves. This dual function is even
embodied in the term *dharma*, which (as we have already seen) for
Buddhism means both things themselves (what really is) and Buddhist
teachings (what Buddhism says about what is). Both meanings are
necessary. To dwell only on the instrumental and referential aspect of
language overlooks the *ippō-gūjin* of words; yet to emphasize only *ippō-
gūjin* ignores the ability of words to affect the way we perceive things
"in" the world. That latter function is also crucial for Buddhism because
Buddhism as a religion is primarily concerned with helping us change
our way of living in the world, which is usually *duḥkha*, dissatisfied.
Śākyamuni Buddha said that he taught only *duḥkha* and the end of
duḥkha.

Distinguishing these two inseparable aspects of language enables us
to clarify the differences between Buddhism and Derrida. On the one
side, Derrida's writings are not aware of the *ippō-gūjin* aspect of
language. From a Hua-yen perspective, it may be said that Derrida
demonstrates how each linguistic-*dharma* is an effect of all other *dharmas*,
but he overlooks the other aspect equally essential for Mahāyāna: that
each linguistic-*dharma* is at the same time the only *dharma* in the whole
universe. Yes, every signification is a function of a network of
differences, yet for that very reason each transient produced effect is also
an end in itself, in fact the only end in itself, the sole reason that the
cosmos exists.[24]

Perhaps a favorite metaphor may be used to illustrate this point. The
musicological analysis of a score may reveal interesting and important
things about the text, but that analysis can never convey the living
experience of listening to that music, of actually hearing (for example)
that climactic moment in classical sonata-form when the key returns to
the dominant and the tension that has been building up is resolved
harmonically. Yet there are also different ways of hearing that harmonic
resolution. Although we usually retain a sense of ourselves as enjoying
the music, there are those all-too-rare moments when we forget ourselves

---

[24] *On Grammatology* privileges writing as a better metaphor for understanding
language than the supposed self-presence of speech. Yet speech remains a better
metaphor for the *ippō-gūjin* of language. Of course, speech does give us an illusion of
wholeness and unity, but the point of *ippō-gūjin* is that that is not *merely* an illusion.
There is more on this argument in the two sources cited in fn. 21.

and *become* the music, when we forget past and future to regain a no-longer-falling-away "eternal now" that flows, as notes no longer succeed each other but the same note dances up and down. This reveals the nondual *ippō-gūjin* of music, which at that moment is not different from our own "empty" nature.

Words and symbols can be *ippō-gūjin* as well because as well as instrumental they are, like music and everything else, groundless: that is, without any self-nature or self-presence, which fact Mahāyāna expresses with the term *śūnya* "empty". From a Buddhist perspective, our intellectual quest may be seen to derive from a sublimated version of the same *duḥkha* that haunts the rest of our lives; in response, we try to fixate ourselves somewhere, if only (for intellectuals like us) on some produced linguistic effect. But as all our various searches for unconditioned grounds and origins are doomed to fail, our philosophizing too sails in an unfathomable ocean without any permanent harbors to cast anchor in. It is only when language is not used as a way to compensate for my own groundlessness—which makes me grasp at it in order to try to get some truth *from* it—that language can become a way the mind consummates itself.

We might want to say that this epiphany involves more than a dance with words, but we can just as well call it a special kind of dance. The playfulness of Hui-neng, Dōgen and Eckhart is an end in itself, to be sure, yet it also embodies an understanding of our *duḥkha* and is a considered response to our *duḥkha*. The deconstructions of dualisms that we find in these religious innovators can help to free us from our own "mind-forg'd manacles" (as Blake put it), from chains of our own making (the Zen metaphor). For Buddhism, and apparently for Eckhart as well, the most important dualism that needs to be deconstructed is that between myself "inside" and the rest of the world "outside". We have noticed how Dōgen devises numerous linguistic devices to subvert the usual dualisms of language, to make language reveal instead the nonduality between us and the world. Eckhart does the same when, for example, he changes "thy will be done" into "will, be thine", and when he refuses to grant being both to God and to creatures at the same time.

Their projects are religious, and Derrida's is not, because this other aspect of language—which works to deconstruct the *duḥkha* of our lives—is also lacking in Derrida. Derrida in effect deconstructs the subject-object opposition by disseminating it, because he does not believe that it can be recuperated or regathered, for we have no access to any nonduality prior to that duality.[25] As a consequence, his deconstruction is more focussed on the *duḥkha* that operates in language, which is the place we intellectuals search for a truth to fixate on; his philosophical critique does not address the role of grasping and fixation in the rest of our lives. Dōgen's Buddhism and Eckhart's Christianity are religions because they offer much broader critiques of attachment intended to inform and alter the ways we live "in" the world. Buddhist usage of language and claims about language are part of a larger, indeed holistic practice—including moral precepts, ritual, meditation exercises, etc.— that develops nonattachment in all our activities and is therefore able to discover and liberate the *ippō-gūjin* in all of them.

IV

In conclusion, we can distinguish not only between dead words and living words, as (in very different ways) Tung-shan and Derrida do, but also between living words and healing words.

We know dead words well enough. The problem with academic discourse is that it flattens language into the one-dimensionality of objectified texts. Our intellectual concern to study and dissect such texts "rigorously" makes this type of discourse paradigmatic for us. The ability to do this well, or cleverly, has become the academic meal-ticket: those who play the game skillfully get published and invited to conferences.

The fact that this is the dwelling-place within language where we have learned to dwell comfortably, and which helps us get tenure, does not deny the other possibilities of language. One such possibility is the dissemination exemplified by Derrida's type of deconstruction and now practiced by many other postmodern writers, not usually so skillfully. That language is certainly more alive than the chess-board rearrangement of jargon predominant in academia. Nonetheless I find something lacking in most of it. One way to express it is that, when merely an end in itself, grammatological freedom quickly becomes boring, like those postmodern novels I can never quite finish, which are stylistically very ingenious yet seem to have little else to communicate besides celebrating their cleverness in transgressing conventional forms.

---

[25] I am indebted to Professor Caputo for this felicitous way of expressing the difference (in a personal communication).

Such vitality should not be confused with the nondual *ippō-gūjin* that Dōgen describes and Eckhart also exemplifies. The deconstructions and disseminations we find in Hui-neng, Dōgen and Eckhart are certainly playful, yet they gain their force—a power that survives through the centuries to touch us today—from their ability to rub against the grain of our *duḥkha*, from their challenge to the deadened categories and automatized dualisms which structure the ways we live and suffer in the world.

Sky-dancing
at the Boundaries of Western Thought

FEMINIST THEORY AND THE LIMITS OF DECONSTRUCTION

PHILIPPA BERRY
KING'S COLLEGE CAMBRIDGE

My aim in this paper is to explore the implications for Western spirituality and religion of certain recurring figures or tropes which occur within deconstruction in particular and in postmodern thought in general: tropes which are gendered feminine. The close relationship between deconstruction and postmodern thought has been much discussed; certainly deconstruction conforms very closely to Jean-François Lyotard's definition of what is postmodern: "The postmodern would be that which, in the modern, puts forward the unpresentable in presentation itself; that which denies itself the solace of good forms...that which searchs for new presentations, not in order to enjoy them, but in order to impart a stronger sense of the unpresentable."[1] Although deconstructive and postmodern thinking may appear to take to an extreme that skeptical style of thinking which has dominated Western society since the Enlightenment, it is because of this pervasive fascination with "the unrepresentable" that I consider both deconstruction in particular and postmodern thought in general to have the potential to transform the imbalanced secularism as well as the unhealthy dualism of contemporary Western thought. However, it is the extension and simultaneous "differing" of key deconstructive or postmodern themes in the work of certain feminist theorists which is most clearly delineating the relevance of this thought to those interested in spirituality and religion, while at the same time revealing important limitations within these theories which leading male exponents of the deconstructive agenda seem currently unable to overcome.

---

[1] Jean-François Lyotard, *The Postmodern Condition: a Report on Knowledge*, trans. Geoff Bennington and Brian Massumi (Manchester: Manchester University Press, 1984), 81.

Deconstruction has recently been much concerned with questions of ethics, and specifically with the issue of the ethical relationship to another/others; yet its continuing implicit refusal to dialogue with those feminist thinkers who are working in a broadly deconstructionist idiom is an eloquent testimony to the blindness of its key exponents not only to what could be the wider ethical and practical significance of their theory, but also to the almost uncanny autonomy of their privileged feminine tropes. Thus what I will examine in this paper is the extension of a feminist "overcoming" of the unacknowledged limitations of deconstruction in the two apparently opposed directions of bodily and spiritual experience—directions which are however closely related. Not only are feminist thinkers able to offer important insights into the relationship between thought and experience, mind and body; by redeploying the feminine motifs of deconstruction with a feminist difference they are also helping to clarify the relationship of questions of spirit to the contemporary theoretical agenda—at a time when the implicit parallels between postmodernism and certain aspects of Eastern as well as Western mysticism are beginning to be widely commented on.

The American feminist and legal theorist Drucilla Cornell has recently redescribed deconstruction as "a philosophy of the limit", and has stressed the importance of its current redirection of intellectual attention to the limits which constrain Western philosophical understanding. Of this disturbing encounter with the boundaries of our inherited models of knowledge, Cornell writes as follows:

> To run into an aporia, to reach the *limit* of philosophy, is not necessarily to
> be paralyzed....The dead end of the aporia, the impasse to which it takes us,
> promises through its prohibition the way out it seems to deny.[2]

The conclusions which Cornell herself draws from this insight are somewhat different from the points which I want to make in this paper. Not only are they specifically allied to her feminist and deconstructive reassessment of legal theory; they are also wholly unconcerned with the half-concealed preoccupation with the sacred which often informs contemporary theoretical interest in alterity or difference. Nonetheless, it is interesting to note that, like many thinkers engaged with deconstruction and postmodern thought, Cornell sees this encounter with "philosophy's limit" as inextricably allied to what Jacques Derrida

---

[2] Drucilla Cornell, *The Philosophy of The Limit* (London and New York: Routledge, 1992), 70-1.

described (as early as 1968) as "the end of man".[3] For as many feminist theorists have pointed out, what is currently being called into play in the implicitly masculine subject by deconstruction is persistently figured in feminine terms. Thus Alice Jardine has commented: "It has become increasingly difficult to find a major theoretician in France today who is not concerned in one way or another with "woman", the "feminine", or variations thereof....The "feminine" has become—to use an old expression of Roland Barthes—a metaphor without brakes.[4] Some of the most notable examples of this postmodern interest in the use of feminine figures appear in the work of Derrida: they include *différance* (in*Writing and Difference)* the feathery pen or *plume*, and the *hymen (Dissemination)*, *chora (Psyché)*, *glas (Glas)* and the trace as cinder or *cendre (Cinders)*.

Of this intriguing trend within contemporary theory, Rosi Braidotti has observed:

> Is it not strange that the reflection on the feminine is so closely connected to a masculine disorder, to the 'death of man', meant as the questioning not only of philosophical truth but of knowledge? For it is in part thanks to this crossing into the void, this phenomenal acting-out on the part of the philosophical subject, that the problematic of the feminine has been given status, as the carrier of a 'new' truth. It is as if the modern subject, the split subject, discovers the feminine layer of his own thought just as he loses the mastery he used to assume as his own.[5]

Braidotti's suggestion that the new thought, in its encounter with a repressed feminine layer of identity, is "crossing into the void", has no overt religious significance for her. But when considered from a mystical perspective, these concepts of emptiness and the loss of identity assume an especial importance. Since the void, space and emptiness are indeed recurring motifs in this body of thought, my essay will consider what might be signified by this feminine dimension of the "end of man" when it is viewed from a broadly religious perspective. I hope that interpretation from this unfamiliar angle will give new meaning to the intellectual aporia or limit which we are now facing in much of the humanities and social sciences.

---

[3] See Jacques Derrida, "The Ends of Man," in *Margins of Philosophy*, trans. Alan Bass (Brighton: Harvester Press, 1982), 109-136. The paper was first given at a international colloquium in New York in October 1968.
[4] Alice Jardine, *Gynesis: configurations of woman and modernity* (Ithaca: Cornell University Press, 1985), 34.
[5] Rosi Braidotti, *Patterns of Dissonance: a study of women in contemporary philosophy*, trans. Elizabeth Guild (Cambridge: Polity Press, 1991), 10.

In an essay which anticipates some of the concerns of Cornell's book, and which was translated into English as "Beyond Aporia", the French philosopher and feminist Sarah Kofman has suggested that:

> The aporetic state always arises as one moves from a familiar environment or space to a space where one is unaccustomed, during a *transition* from below to above or from above to below, from darkness to light or from light to darkness....There can be no aporia, in the true sense of the word, without a transition from a familiar state which affords one every security to a new, and therefore harrowing, state.[6]

The importance attributed to desire as the impulse which most commonly impels one across or **beyond** the boundaries established by the intellect, and into a disturbing encounter with nothingness, is perhaps nowhere more vividly expressed in twentieth-century thought than in the writings of Georges Bataille, for whom to take *le pas au-delà*—that is, to go beyond the limits of rational knowledge—was an act of transgression intimately related to the experience of erotic desire or *jouissance*. In *Visions of Excess*, Bataille gives a graphic description of arrival at this threshold: "there he [sic] must throw himself headlong into that which has no foundation and no head".[7] It is significant that Bataille here attributes the masculine gender to the one experiencing this sensation; elsewhere in his work, this leap or fall into nothingness is specifically related to an encounter with an idea of woman as Other:

> ELLE is nothing, there is nothing sensible in ELLE, not even finally darkness. In ELLE, everything fades away, but, exorbitant, I traverse an empty depth and an empty depth traverses me. In ELLE, I communicate with the 'unknown'... [8]

Yet this memorable exposition of woman's affinity with nothingness is not wholly original to Bataille, for it expands upon the ideas of a thinker who, in his opposition to rationalism, is often termed the founding father of deconstruction, and whose aphoristic remarks about women have recently become almost as influential as those of Freud: Nietzsche. It was Nietzsche, of course, whose critique of the privileged masculine construction of truth in Western thought led him to ask "supposing

---

[6] Sarah Kofman, "Beyond Aporia", in *Post-structuralist classics*, ed. Andrew Benjamin (London: Routledge, 1989), 19-21.
[7] Georges Bataille, *Visions of Excess: Selected Writings 1927-1939*, trans. A. Stoekl (Manchester: Manchester University Press, 1985), 222.
[8] Bataille, *Inner Experience*, trans. Leslie Anne Boldt (Albany, NY: SUNY Press, 1988), 125.

Truth is a woman—what then?"[9] and who claimed that "There is no essence of woman, because she diverts herself, and is diverted from herself".[10] These observations, mediated to an important extent by the work of Bataille, have clearly influenced the figuration of woman in Derridean deconstruction; commenting in a work entitled *Spurs* upon Nietzsche's account of woman as emptiness and untruth, Derrida remarks: "Here philosophical discourse, blinded, founders, and allows itself to be hurled down to its ruin".[11]

The value and importance of these Nietzschean observations for a feminist engagement with deconstruction and postmodernism is currently being stressed by a number of thinkers[12]; yet ironically, for Nietzsche, this idea of woman as insubstantial, illusory, remained profoundly disturbing. In fact, his failure to elaborate its implications could be seen as one of the fundamental flaws in a system which elsewhere celebrated a Dionysian principle of *ek-stasis*, for the affinities of this concept with the feminine (as much as with the oriental or the non-Greek) are only too apparent from any cursory examination of Greek mythology—and especially of Euripides' *The Bacchae*. Similarly, while Derridean deconstruction appears at one level to be profoundly influenced by feminist critiques, both of the excessively rational masculine subjectivity which is currently in crisis, and of the dualistic model of knowledge which it has privileged, its refusal properly to acknowledge feminist thinkers arguably signifies a failure of that compassionate response to "the Other" which is stressed by Emmanuel Levinas, who has reminded us that "the absolutely foreign alone can instruct us".[13] Accordingly it seems symptomatic of the male thinker's failure to convert deconstructive *theoria* into a healing *praxis*.

---

[9] Friedrich Nietzsche, *Beyond Good and Evil*, trans. W. Kaufmann (New York: Random House, 1968), Preface, p. 1.

[10] Nietzsche, *The Joyful Wisdom* , trans. W. Kaufmann (New York: Frederic Ungar, 1960), 38/48.

[11] Derrida, *Spurs/Eperons*, trans. Barbara Harlow, intro. Stefano Agosti (Chicago: University of Chicago Press, 1976), 51.

[12] Jean Graybeal, *Language and the Feminine in Nietzsche and Heidegger* (Bloomington, Indiana: Indiana University Press, 1990); Joke J. Hermsen, "Baubo or Bacchante? Sarah Kofman and Nietzsche's affirmative woman" in *Sharing the Difference: feminist debates in Holland*, eds. Joke J. Hermsen and Alkeline van Lenning (London: Routledge, 1992); David Farrell Krell, *Postponements: woman, sensuality and death in Nietzsche* (Bloomington, Indiana: Indiana University Press, 1986); Susan J. Hekman, *Gender and Knowledge* (Cambridge: Polity Press, 1992).

[13] Emmanuel Levinas, *Totality and Infinity*, trans. Alphonso Lingis (Pittsburgh, Penn.: Duquesne University Press, 1969), 73. It is notable that even in a debate with Christie Macdonald on the subject of feminism and deconstruction, Derrida makes no reference to French feminist thinkers working virtually alongside him—although he does refer there to the work of Emmanuel Levinas! (See "Choreographies", in *The Ear*

Yet perhaps this resistance, of Derrida as well as Nietzsche, is rather more comprehensible when it is viewed through the lens of French feminism. This highly philosophical strand of feminist thought is often criticised for its essentialist conceptions of woman; but in fact, a number of its key thinkers, notably Julia Kristeva, Luce Irigaray and Hélène Cixous, have developed sophisticated accounts of the specifically feminist implications of the deconstructive idea of woman's "non-existence" or "nothingness". These accounts comment on and explain the fear which it still appears to inspire in most of those male thinkers who attempt to theorize it. Thus Julia Kristeva, taking her cue from Bataille as well as from Freud, Melanie Klein, and Jacques Lacan, has illuminated the relationship between those psychic forces which are experienced as menacing the linguistic control of the ego or subjectivity and our earliest relationship with the mother, through an extended discussion of the Platonic term *chora*. As redescribed by Kristeva in the context of psychoanalysis, this is an originary psychic space which is essentially non-discursive, yet is both rhythmic and highly mobile:

> In the meaning of Plato, *chora* designates a mobile receptacle in which things are mixed, a place of contradiction and movement, necessary to the operation of nature before the teleological intervention of God, and corresponding to the mother: the *chora* is a matrix or a nurse in which the elements have no identity and no purpose. The *chora* is the *locus* of a *chaos* which *is* and which *becomes*, previous to the formation of the first definite bodies.[14]

Kristeva emphasises that *chora*'s primordial character represents a dangerous threat to the stability of the ego or the I: "The place of the subject's creation, the semiotic *chora* is also the place of its negation, where its unity gives way before the process of charges and stases producing that unity."[15] Intimately allied to *chora*, therefore, is a complex mesh of feelings of fear and revulsion which Kristeva terms **abjection**, feelings which seem often to inform cultural hostility to women, but which are merely the other side of *jouissance* or desire—and here she reminds us of the complex interrelationship between the death drive and the pleasure principle which was noted by Freud. Kristeva stresses that the cause of this state (abjection) is: "what disturbs identity, system, order. What does not respect borders, positions, rules. The in-between,

---

of the Other: texts and discussions with Jacques Derrida, ed. Christie Macdonald (Lincoln, Nebraska: University of Nebraska Press, 1987, 163-186.)

[14] Julia Kristeva, *Polylogue* (Paris: Seuil, 1977), 57, n.1 (my translation). For a more detailed description of the concept of *chora* as used by Kristeva, see Elizabeth Grosz, *Sexual Subversions: three French feminists* (London: Allen and Unwin, 1990), chapter 2.

[15] Julia Kristeva, *La révolution du langage poétique* (Paris: Seuil, 1974), 27.

the ambiguous, the composite."[16] What these feelings repeat, Kristeva contends, are our earliest attempts "to release the hold of *maternal entity*".[17] The abject consequently "takes the ego back to its source on the abominable limits from which, in order to be, the ego has broken away"[18], because it challenges the subject-object dichotomy upon which rational meaning (and language) depends, and reminds the ego of the lack and flux upon which it is founded. Especially relevant to the concerns of this essay is Kristeva's observation that "[a]bjection accompanies all religious structurings and reappears, to be worked out in a new guise, at the time of their collapse".[19] She also notes that the state of abjection frequently causes the ego or I to perceive the loathed image as *unheimlich(e)*, or uncanny.

As theorized by Kristeva, moreover, it seems that the abject is intimately related to endings as well as to beginnings; while she allies abjection closely with the Freudian concept of "primal repression", and hence with the ambivalent feelings experienced by the child towards the mother at the point at which it is struggling to form a separate identity, she also posits the corpse as the image which most typically inspires abjection in adult life: "the corpse, the most sickening of wastes, is a border that has encroached upon everything".[20] Yet Kristeva also contends that the challenge posed to the ego by abjection is "an alchemy that transforms death drive into a start of life, of new significance".[21] While her interpretation of this new beginning is quite strictly defined within the framework of psychoanalytic theory, the implications of her perspective are, in my view, much more far-reaching.

Kristeva emphasises abjection's liminal character, its disrespect of borders; similarly, Kofman has contended that "aporia...breaks with the logic of identity, and...pertains to the logic of the intermediary".[22] And although deconstruction is by no means original in its association of the idea of woman with that otherness which is excluded from the dominant model of knowledge, and which it frequently represents as a disturbing nothingness, an **abyss** threatening to destroy resemblance and the self (categories which have implicit associations with masculinity at the present epoch), both Derrida and several French feminist thinkers have also shown that in an important sense, and perhaps especially at this

[16] Julia Kristeva, *Powers of Horror: an essay on abjection* (New York: Columbia University Press, 1982), 4.
[17] Ibid., 13.
[18] Ibid., 15.
[19] Ibid., 17.
[20] Ibid., 3.
[21] Ibid., 15.
[22] Kofman, "Beyond Aporia", 27.

historical conjuncture, the concept of woman partakes of the attributes of the **inbetween** place, space or boundary, which paradoxically unites and undoes binary oppositions even while it appears to maintain them. This is the implication, for example, of Derrida's curious feminine motif of the *hymen* as a key factor in the operation of that "spacing" which he terms the differ*a*nce in a text:

> The virginity of the *"yet unwritten page"* opens up that space...To repeat: the hymen, the confusion between the present and the nonpresent, along with all the indifferences it entails within the whole series of opposites..., produces the effect of a medium (a medium as element enveloping both terms at once; a medium located between the two terms). It is an operation that *both* sows confusion *between* opposites *and* stands *between* the opposites "at once". What counts here is the *between*, the in-between-ness of the hymen. The hymen "takes place" in the "inter-", in the spacing between desire and fulfillment, between perpetration and its recollection. But this medium of the *entre* has nothing to do with a center.[23]

Later in the same text, Derrida plays persistently on the feathery mobility of the pen as *plume* by punning on *elle* and *aile* ("her" and "wing"). His implication seems to be that this feminine "in-between-ness" has an aerial as well as a textual dimension.

French feminism has consciously positioned itself in the ambiguous feminine space opened up by Derrida and others, expanding thereby the dynamic implications of this indeterminate location. Simultaneously, it has invested it with a quasi-religious character. For example, the intimate connection of *chora* both with bodily expression and gesture and with a social commentary which has close affinities with "the gods", is suggested by Kristeva's later comparision of this "dancing receptacle" to the chorus of Greek drama, in an essay on the painter Jackson Pollock. And while in her essay "Motherhood according to Bellini" she stressed the Virgin Mary's affinity with an "Oriental nothingness", in another essay, "Stabat Mater", she also drew attention to the Virgin's mystical function as a "bond", "middle" and "interval".[24] But it is in the works of Cixous and Irigaray that Derrida's imagery of feathers and wings has been accorded a new feminist as well as spiritual significance: on the one hand, by the association of these motifs with a revisioning of the female mystic or saint (like Kristeva's work on the Virgin Mary); on the other

---

[23] Jacques Derrida, *Dissemination*, trans. Barbara Johnson (London: Athlone Press, 1981), 212.
[24] Julia Kristeva, "Motherhood according to Bellini", in *Desire in Language*, trans. and ed. Leon S. Roudiez *et al.* (Oxford: Blackwell, 1990), 247; "Stabat Mater", in *The Kristeva Reader*, ed. Toril Moi (Oxford, Blackwell, 1986), 162.

hand, by the elaboration of feminist versions of flight and of angelic identity.

For Cixous, a novelist who is also an academic and feminist theorist, the spacing opened up within texts by deconstruction's questioning of the authority of the I or "subject" over their text is one which enables the feminist writer to "voler"—to steal from her cultural heritage in order to remake it, and so to fly or take flight (both being additional senses of "voler") into a spacious freedom. The female author of Cixous's work is therefore like an acrobat who no longer needs her trapeze, since she has discovered that: "I am myself the trapeze and the trapezist".[25] Elsewhere, Cixous tropes the articulation of a feminist difference in writing as an angelic visitation to the woman writer, associating this event with an empoverishing of the self that echoes the espousal of Lady Poverty in Franciscan mysticism:

> This night the writing came to me,—Clarice, her angel's footsteps in my room....the stroke of truth in the desert my room. My angel struggled with me; my angel of poverty called me, its voice Clarice, the inebriant call of poverty. I struggled, she read me, in the fire of her writing.[26]

In fact, a pun which recurs through much of Cixous's work suggests that it is only when the "I" of the authorial self is displaced and put into question, *en-jeu* , that the angel as *ange* can be realised.

Luce Irigaray has a similar conception of angels as occupying that space of mediation and differance which has been opened up by Derridean deconstruction. Stressing the angel's "whiteness and transparency" (which evokes the "virginity" of Derrida's "white spaces"), she has redefined the female body as a container or envelope which is capable of opening to the space between (whether between lovers, or between heaven and earth), and so to the motions of both air and angels:

> The angel is that which unceasingly passes through the envelopes or containers, goes from one side to the other, reworking every deadline, changing every decision, thwarting all representations. Angels destroy the

---

[25] Hélène Cixous, *LA* (Paris: des femmes, 1976). In this respect Cixous (as well as Irigaray) accords the female subject a greater freedom than does Rosi Braidotti, in her use of a similar metaphor: "The nomadic style of thinking that I advocate as a new feminist position requires the talents of a tightrope-walker, an acrobat....For if Ariadne has fled from the labyrinth of old, the only guiding thread for all of us now, women and men alike, is a tightrope stretched above the void." (Braidotti, *Patterns*, 15.)
[26] Hélène Cixous, *Vivre l'oranje* (Paris: des femmes, 1979), 42.

> monstrous, that which hampers the birth of a new age; they come to herald the arrival of a new birth, a new morning....
>
> These swift angelic messengers, who transgress all envelopes in their speed, tell of the passage between the envelope of God and that of the world as micro- or macrocosm. They proclaim that such a journey can be made by the body of man, and above all the body of woman.[27]

In the framework of religious belief, of course, it is the saint or mystic who is especially responsive to the messages of angels; in this respect, the "other woman" to which Irigaray's philosophy attempts to give shape is always already a mystic. Certainly, in identifying with one who communicates with and becomes like angels, Irigaray appears to be echoing some of the preoccupations of early Christian monasticism as well as reconsidering the event of the Annunciation (and while Kristeva does not specifically mention angels, her focus on the Virgin Mary hints at a similar concern); in recent works, Irigaray's emphasis upon the wisdom of silence and of the breath certainly bespeaks a fascination with the Christian tradition of contemplation as well as with Eastern techniques of meditation.[28] But the mystical female figure who is implicit in so much of Irigaray's work is ultimately a figure of the present and the future rather than of the past, for she is closely involved with those painful processes of cultural and social change which inform deconstruction and postmodern theory, in which man is contemplating his end.

In the sceptical framework of much contemporary Western thought, both the notion of an absolute intellectual boundary and the hypothesis of the "end of man" typically evoke the imagery of death: it is this recognition which has presumably led Derrida to stress the intimate relationship between deconstruction and the activity of mourning in several of his recent works. Thus deconstruction has positioned itself in relation to a variety of funereal landscapes—the tomb, the place of execution, the cremation ground or cemetery.[29] In such scenarios, the oblique associations between an abjected and liminal idea of woman and the horror of death are frequently apparent—in the *la* or "her" embedded at the centre of Derrida's *glas* or death-knell, for example, as

---

[27] Irigaray, *Ethics*, 15.

[28] See for example *L'Oubli de l'air chez Martin Heidegger* (Paris: Minuit, 1983), and *Essere Due* (Turin: Bollati Boringhieri, 1994).

[29] See much of the work of Bataille and of Maurice Blanchot; Julia Kristeva, *Powers of Horror*, op. cit., and *Black Sun: mourning and melancholia* (1990); and Derrida, *Glas*, trans. John P. Leavey and Richard Rand (Lincoln, Nebraska and London: University of Nebraska Press, 1986), *Cinders*, trans. Ned Lukacher (Lincoln, Nebraska and London: University of Nebraska Press, 1991), *Memoires for Paul de Man* (New York: Columbia University Press, 1986).

well as in the figurative associations between woman, ash, and a place of burning (*là*) drawn out in *Cinders* (or *Feu là cendre*). In the notes to *Cinders*, Derrida briefly alludes to the fiery death of a female heretic of the late middle ages, Marguérite Porete; yet Irigaray had associated the transgressive desires of the female mystic (and, I have suggested elsewhere, of Porete in particular) with burning as early as *Speculum of the Other Woman*:

> This is the place where "she"—and in some cases he, if he follows "her" lead—speaks about the dazzling glare which comes from the source of light that has been logically repressed, about "subject" and "Other" flowing out into an embrace of fire that mingles one term into another, about contempt for form as such, about mistrust for understanding as an obstacle along the path of jouissance and mistrust for the dry desolation of reason. Also about a burning glass. This is the only place in the history of the West in which woman speaks and acts so publicly. [30]

Later, in *An Ethics of Sexual Difference*, she anticipates: "A new Pentecost, when fire—mingled perhaps with wind—will be given back to the female so that a world still to come can be accomplished."[31] In her own revisioning of *Revelation*, Irigaray anticipates a union of the fiery Holy Spirit (whose gender, significantly, she never specifies) with the feminine as Bride—a union in which body and spirit, earth and heaven, will be reunited. In this utopian expectation of a third age of the Spirit, she appears to align herself quite explicitly with the Joachimite mysticism of the middle ages, and draws out what for her appear to be its feminist implications:

> The spirit is not to be imprisoned only in the Father-son duality. The spirit eludes this "couple". This event is announced in the Gospel itself: the females, the women, partake not in the Last Supper but in the Pentecost, and it is they who discover and announce the resurrection. This seems to say that the body of man can return to life when woman no longer forgets that she has a share in the spirit..." [32]

---

[30] Luce Irigaray, *Speculum of the Other Woman*, trans. Gillian C. Gill (Ithaca: Cornell University Press, 1985), "La Mystérique". The centrality of the female mystic to this text is discussed in Philippa Berry, "The Burning Glass: paradoxes of feminist revelation in *Speculum*, in *Engaging with Iragaray*, eds. Carolyn Burke *et al.* (New York: Columbia University Press, 1994).

[31] *Ethics*, 147.

[32] Ibid., 149. The impact of the eschatological writings of Joachim of Fiore upon late medieval mysticism and heresy has now been widely discussed. See for example Robert E. Lerner, *Heresy of the Free Spirit in the Later Middle Ages* (Berkeley, Calif.:

Certainly, the focus of all of these women thinkers upon the different and liminal wisdom of women, and that which it can offer to diverse forms of dogma, has no specific parallel in Christian tradition, unless it be in the various female heretics of the middle ages. Those female mystics who won Church validation, in contrast to women like Marguérite Porete, achieved this only at a price. Only in the very recent past has the radical difference of women's voices begun to be heard and acknowledged within Christian tradition, in the discourse of feminist theology. In speculating upon the difference represented by the writings of these French feminists within the deconstructive tradition, therefore, we may also begin to learn something about the potential of feminist theology. But in conclusion, and in order to suggest some of the ways in which a spacious feminine difference may have the potential to transform an intellectual system—and a model of identity—which has reached a seemingly impassable limit, I will use an analogy to Vajrāyāna Buddhism, for in spite of what is sometimes considered to be its patriarchal structure, this branch of Buddhism has traditionally valued the difference of certain "angelic" feminine voices in matters of vital spiritual guidance.

It is of course in the macabre setting of the funereal burning-ground that several of the Buddhist *mahā-siddhas* (or *sgrub-tob*) who were to shape the Vajrāyāna tradition are described as encountering the fearsome female beings called *ḍākinīs* (or *mkha'gromas*).[33] In the biographies of the *mahā-siddhas*, these encounters were represented as inspiring and directing their revolutionary deviations from the overly intellectual and custom-bound practices of the monasteries of Mahāyāna Buddhism, where devotion to the Sūtras, and to doctrine, had apparently come to supercede meditation in importance.[34] What typically resulted from such a meeting was devotion to a nomadic life which (in an intriguing paradox) combined wandering with long periods of solitary meditation, which were now organized around a new kind of *sādhana* or contemplative practice. This led in turn to the reception and elaboration of the tantras, and the establishment of the Vajrāyāna path to enlightenment.

University of California Press, 1972) and Marjorie Reeves, *Joachim of Fiore and the Prophetic Future* (London: SPCK, 1976).

[33] This practice was in fact also favoured by the Indian sadhus, as well as (according to the *Vinaya-Piṭaka*) by Śākyamuni and his monks, some of whom gathered scraps of cloth for their robes in these locations.

[34] See Abhayadatta, *Buddha's Lions: the lives of the eighty-four siddhas*, trans. James B. Robinson (Berkeley, Calif.: Dharma Publishing, 1979); also Nathan Katz, "Anima and mKha'-'gro-ma: a critical comparative study of Jung and Tibetan Buddhism", *Tibet Journal* (1983), 13-43.

The objective of this religious revolution, which was to attain a clear insight into the essentially **empty** nature of all phenomena, or *śūnyatā*, has an especially close relationship to the Mahāyāna *Prajñāpāramitā* sutras, where the perfection of profound cognition, *prajñāpāramitā* is held to be knowledge of voidness. This supra-intellectual mode of knowing is sometimes equated with wisdom, but Tsultrim Allione has pointed out that in the Kagyu and Nyingmapa traditions *prajñā* (Tib., *Shesrab*) is a tool to **discover** wisdom (*Yeshes*), not wisdom itself.[35] In this sense it could perhaps be described as inspiration. The concept of *prajñā* was personified in a more or less abstract and static (as well as aesthetically pleasing) form by the goddess Prajñāpāramitā in the text of that name. But for the *mahāsiddhas*, its paradoxical physicality or **embodiment** (in a body which is by definition illusory and empty), together with its innate dynamism and mobility (that is, its associations with spiritual energy), were seemingly of much greater importance. It is these qualities of *prajñā* of course, which are stressed in its personification by the dakini, whose Tibetan name identifies her with the ceaseless flux of the void, describing her as a sky-goer, sky-walker or sky-dancer. Hence the characteristic posture of the dakini is dancing. This pose seems to refer to the leap in consciousness to which she invites the practitioner; it also echoes the mobile, indeed choric associations of Kristeva's *chora*. The vajra attributes of the dakini likewise represent that abrupt cutting through of obstacles to enlightenment which is fundamental to the vajra or diamond path—as well as her self-sufficiency/androgyny. This cutting through extends both to academic conceptualizations and to the five *skandhas* or poisons, which are transformed through the seed-syllable HŪM into the five wisdoms of the mandala of the *sambhoghakāya* buddhas.[36] (In the Tibetan visualization practice of *chod* which—perhaps significantly—was introduced by a female practitioner, Machig Lapdron, this incisiveness also extends to the chopping up of the body, as representative of the ego-centrered self).

But at the same time (and not surprisingly, given her association with the burning ground) the process of transformation initiated by the dakini and associated with the HŪM is sometimes figured in terms of her association with the mystic heat or inner fire. This is *gtummo*, one of the yogas of completion, which is described as fusing all polarities. For like other wrathful deities (such as Vajrāpāṇi), she is frequently depicted

[35] Tsultrim Allione, *Women of Wisdom* (London: Routledge and Kegan Paul, 1984), 130, n. 10.
[36] For the importance of HŪM, see Lama Anagarika Govinda, *Foundations of Tibetan Mysticism* (London: Rider, 1987), 129-206. Allione, incidentally, relates the three-pronged trident of the dakini Vajrāvarāhi to the three poisons of passion, anger and ignorance (ibid., 169).

with an aura of flames. This attribute and function of the dakini affords an interesting analogy to the imagery of fire evoked in Irigaray's *Speculum*, as well as to Derrida's comment in *Cinders* concerning *là* as the place of burning—a location in which the emptiness of Being makes itself manifest: "If a place is itself surrounded by fire...it no longer is."[37] If the siddha responds thoughtfully—and compassionately—to the encounter with the dakini, the result seems at one level to be a purification of the ignorance of dualistic thinking. This is replaced by a non-referential mode of thought—a thinking from the heart in which thought is integrally related to compassionate action. It seems a wholly new mode of cognition; but this combination of heart and mind is frequently described as a **return** to an unconditioned, primordial state which is innate in everyone.[38] In the terms of *Mahāmudrā*, this represents, not an abolition or overcoming of negativity, but rather an **integration** of pure with impure vision, an indissoluble unity of *saṃsāra* and *nirvāṇa*. The tantric focus upon the HŪṂ is certainly consistent with such a perspective, since this seed-syllable is often interpreted as grounding the abstract insights of initiation (represented by the OṂ) in the body and lived experience.

The associations of Buddhahood with return to a primordial state analogous to that of the newly-born infant are certainly implicit in the description of the initiation of Padmasambhava, or Guru Rinpoche, by the chief of the dakinis, in canto 34 of the biography attributed to his chief consort, the dakini Yeshe Tsogyal. This describes his visit to "the cemetery of sleep in the mysterious paths of beatitude". Here the "precious guru" has a preliminary encounter with the chief dakini's maidservant, herself a dakini, outside the closed door of "the castle of the skull" (this is presumably a reference to the dakini's typical attribute of a skullcap filled with blood). When the maidservant cuts open her chest with a crystal knife, Padmasambhava is shown the hidden inner nature of corporeality, for her body mysteriously contains the mandalas of the peaceful and wrathful deities. This insight into the body as both empty and simultaneously the means of enlightenment, prepares him for entrance into the castle (which is a culmination of his long contemplation of death, in so many cemeteries!); also for incorporation into the body of

---

[37] *Cinders*, op. cit., 36. On the imagery of fire in *Speculum*, see my essay "The burning glass", op. cit.

[38] While this primordial ground of being is strictly speaking ungendered, just as is the phallic mother of the pre-oedipal stage as described by Kristeva, it is often referred to as "*Yum Chenmo*", "the Great Mother". Chogyam Trungpa wrote of it as follows: "As a principle of cosmic stucture, the all-accomodating basic ground is neither male nor female, one might call it hermaphroditic, but due to its quality of fertility and potentiality it is regarded as feminine". (*Maitreya* IV, 23-4).

the chief dakini, for he is **swallowed** in response to his request for "the Teachings, outer, inner, and secret":

> The bhikṣuni spoke:

> "You understand in your request for power that all the gods are gathered in my heart."
> She then changed Dorje Drolod [alias Padmasambhava] into the syllable HŪṂ
> and swallowed him, thus conferring blessings upon him.
> Outwardly his body become like that of the Buddha Amitabha,
> and he obtained the powers of the Knowledge Bearer of Life.
> From the blessings of being within her body,
> inwardly his body become that of Avalokiteśvara,
> and he obtained the powers of the meditation of the Great Seal [Mahāmudrā].
> He was then, with blessings, ejected through her secret lotus,
> and his body, speech, and mind were thus purified from mental defilements.
> Secretly his body became that of Hayagrīva, Being of power,
> and he obtained the power of binding the highest gods and genies.[39]

The comparison of our contemporary intellectual situation in the West to events which took place in northwest India sometime between the fourth and ninth centuries CE may seem somewhat farfetched, and certainly the parallels between the two situations are by no means exact. Most importantly, we live in a predominantly secular and nihilistic society, in radical contrast to the religiosity of India in its great era of Buddhist flowering. So what can our twentieth-century graveyard meditations, as Western philosophers think "the end of thinking" amidst postmodern scenarios of dereliction and waste, find in common with those of these oriental supermen? Cornell has indicated very clearly in *The Philosophy of the Limit* that along with other related facets of postmodern thought, deconstruction is currently much preoccupied with the issue of ethics: in other words, with that thorny question which I raised earlier, of the relationship of its elegant and erudite theory to social practice. The position of the deconstructionist might thus not unreasonably be compared to that of a *mahā-siddha*-to-be such as Nāropa, who when abbot of Nālandā monastery had to admit to the dakini Vajrāvarāhi that he knew the **words**, but not the **meaning** of the doctrines which he studied, and who subsequently went in search of the "brother of the dakini", Tilopa, in order to learn that which his

---

[39] *The Life and Liberation of Padmasambhava*, by Yeshe Tsogyal, trans. into French by Gustave-Charles Toussaint (1912), into English by Kenneth Douglas and Gwendolen Bays (Berkeley, Calif.: Dharma Press, 1978), vol. 1, 220–1.

monastery could not teach him. *The Life and Teaching of Nāropa* emphasizes that the wisdom conferred by Tilopa is that of the dakini, for the guru repeatedly tells Nāropa to "[l]ook into the mirror of your mind...The mysterious home of the Ḍākinī".[40]

The encounter with the dakini consequently appears to function as the ultimate stage in the *mahā-siddha*'s quest for the perfection of wisdom. The achievement of direct, experiential insight into her essentially empty nature is indeed the most notable (although not the only) method by which the siddha obtains the ultimate siddhi, Buddhahood, and overcomes death. In this respect, we could say that Vajrayana Buddhism achieved a union of theory and practice that Western thought, which is concerned with versions of nothingness or emptiness, has yet to accomplish. It did this, paradoxically, by embracing a figure which at first sight seems grotesquely different and opposed to its inherited teachings. Perhaps it was his hesitation on just this count that vitiated Nietzsche's deconstruction of rationalism, together with his quest for a new, superhuman, model of identity. For when compared to the themes of Tantric Buddhism, his several descriptions of the philosopher of the future dancing on the abyss evoke nothing so clearly as the sky-walkers themselves. Nietzsche wrote of his new science in *The Joyful Wisdom:*

> he [sic] who is accustomed to it may live nowhere else save in this light, transparent, powerful and electric air....In this clear, strict element he has his power whole: here, he can fly! [41]

And he hypothesised that:

> ...one could imagine a delight and a power of self-determining, and a freedom of will, whereby a spirit could bid farewell to every belief, to every wish for certainty, accustomed as it would be to support itself on slender cords and possibilities, and to dance even on the verge of abysses. [42]

The striking character of this analogy suggests to me that if our Western philosophers of the limit are to discover the experiential meaning of deconstruction, they may have to become rather more attentive to feminist thinkers, some of whom are already beginning to perform something akin to that philosophic dance in space which was envisaged by Nietzsche. For while Rosi Braidotti has described

---

[40] *The Life and Teaching of Narapo,* trans. H. Guenther (Oxford: Oxford University Press, 1963).
[41] *The Joyful Wisdom,* op. cit., IV, no. 293, p. 228.
[42] Ibid., V, no. 347, p. 287.

contemporary feminist theorists as "[v]eritable adventuresses into the field of theory...they reveal remarkable acrobatic talents as they trace mental routes across the void, without falling victim to gravity"[43], Luce Irigaray has written that:

> After the envelope full of water which was our prenatal home, we have to construct, bit by bit, the envelope of air of our terrestrial space, air which is still free to breathe and sing, air where we deploy our appearances and movements. We have been fish. We will have to become birds. Which cannot be done without opening up and mobility in the air.[44]

As they discover what might be termed an "unbearable lightness of being", therefore, these feminist theorists seem literally to be a leap ahead of their male counterparts. Yet while their message appears still to be inaudible to other contemporary philosophers, it seems hopeful that religious studies and theology will be better able to ponder the insights of these innovative feminist thinkers, as they sky-dance, intrepidly, at the limits of Western thought.

[43] Braidotti, *Patterns*, 280.

[44] Luce Irigaray, "Divine Women", trans. Stephen Muecke, *Local Consumption: Occasional Papers* 8 (Sydney, 1986), 7.

I am grateful to John Peacocke for his advice concerning research into the figure of the dakini. I would also like to thank Thubten Jinpa, James Low and Leon Redler for their comments on an earlier version of this paper.

Mindfulness of the Selves

THERAPEUTIC INTERVENTIONS IN A TIME OF DIS-SOLUTION

MORNY JOY
THE UNIVERSITY OF CALGARY

Late twentieth-century Western thought seems to be caught in something of a bind. The movement of postmodernism submits all our cherished assumptions, inherited from Greek metaphysics and the Enlightenment, to rigorous and often skeptical scrutiny. The threat of environmental catastrophe poses a monumental challenge that demands a response markedly different from past efforts. Racism, sexism and classism still pervade our social structures in ways that damage the lives of billions of people. Traditional Christianity, aligned in its theological constructs with the problematized state of philosophy, appears ineffectual and limited in its resources for change. Alternative possibilities remain difficult to discern. Can the postmodern tactics of deconstruction with its indefinite conclusions shed any light on the type of procedures necessary to avert a world-wide ecological disaster? Can it provide insight into the dysfunctional patterns of social functioning? What critical resources can be brought to bear on this dire situation? Where is the culprit to be located? One that many sources indict is the notion of the autonomous self that has reigned as the principal paradigm of Western individualism since the Enlightenment.

What are the accusations? Ecologically-minded advocates insist that the all-conquering self is responsible for the present lamentable state of the environment. Feminists, African-Americans, immigrant and other minority groups declare that the dominant and exclusionary practices of this predominantly white, male-identified mode of superiority has prevented their admission to equitable status and access. All parties support a revised understanding of this concept of self. But how can a self be defined in ways that do not encourage mastery and conquest of whatever is deemed different or deficient (by its own measures of self-referentiality)? Postmodern pundits would have us believe that there is no such thing as a self. How can a way be found beyond such an impasse, when such theoretical postulates seem at odds with much needed practical reforms?

This question is particularly crucial in the area of religious studies, where the constitution of a self is seen as intimately related to images of God. As Mark C. Taylor has observed:

> The relation between God and self is thoroughly specular; each mirrors the other. In different terms, man is made in the image of God. This *imago* is an imitation, copy, likeness, representation, similitude, appearance, or shadow of divinity. The *imago dei* confers on man an identity; this establishes a vocation that can be fulfilled only through the process of imitation.[1]

The postmodern approach, with its emphasis on radical discontinuity, questions specifically the notions of God as first cause or as ultimate destination of sentient activity. This conventional view has reinforced the idea of humanity as the dominant species with a vested interest in its image of the lord of creation. Yet postmodernism does not promote any alternative procedure, for "[d]econstruction within theology writes the epitaph for the dead God."[2] Within the Christian legacy, process thought is trying to break with the order of authoritative entitlement, but not in as definitive a way as deconstruction. It shuns static metaphysical categories and linear modes of causality in favor of a kinetic pattern of interacting elements. Feminist and womanist scholars are also exploring alternative modes of defining both God and identity.[3]

---

[1] Mark C. Taylor, *Erring: A Postmodern A/theology* (Chicago: University of Chicago Press, 1984) 35.

[2] Carl A. Raschke, "The Deconstruction of God," *Deconstruction and Theology* (New York: Crossroad, 1982), 27.

[3] In the Christian feminist tradition see Elizabeth A. Johnson, *She Who Is: The Mystery of God in Feminist Theological Discourse* (New York: Crossroad, 1992); Sallie McFague, *Models of God: Theology for an Ecological Nuclear Age* (Philadelphia, Penn.: Fortress Press, 1987), and in the womanist tradition, Jacquelyn Grant, *White Women's Christ and Black Women's Jesus* (Atlanta, Georgia: Scholars Press, 1989); Dolores Williams, *Sisters in the Wilderness: The Challenge of Womanist God-Talk* (Maryknoll: Orbis, 1994). The term *womanist* is the name used by African-American women to distinguish themselves from the white middle-class perspective which has informed much of North American feminism.

As they finally begin to come into their own, should women subscribe to the traditional notion of the self that is being discredited? Or should they align themselves with deconstructive disruptions, only to find themselves back where they started—with their identity still being assigned to them by male theorists, in accordance with the current intellectual fashion? Many women believe their plight is comparable to that of our ecological problem—and that solutions to both these instances of oppression cannot be achieved simply by focusing on environmental issues, for the dominance of nature and women come from the same source. Could ecology, as reconstructed by feminists, have anything further to offer that is of a affirmative nature regarding configurations of self? Finally, with regard to African Americans, minorities and other groups who identify themselves with post-colonial thinking—how can they find a way to assert their rights in ways that do not replicate the hegemonic imposition of an imperial and acquisitive sense of self? Our attempts at defining new insights to replace the superseded abstract notions of God and identity are still in their formative stage.

Perhaps this is where Buddhism can be of assistance, but not without some qualifications and clarifications. Since its origins, Buddhism has been profoundly suspicious of essentialist configurations of identity. Theoretically, this insight is reached in Buddhism by the deflation of substantive pretensions, such as essence and presence, in a manner quite similar to that of the tactics of deconstruction. Yet the Buddhist program also includes specific practices to achieve non-attachment, which draws attention to certain deficiencies in deconstruction. Buddhism, then, may be able to make a more constructive contribution to reformulating a type of self that may promote the requisite new mode of self-awareness and its appropriate application for feminists, ecologists and disenfranchised groups.

In this paper my aim is to examine some of the various options presented by feminist, ecological and minority thinkers—ones that are representative but not exhaustive of the explorations being made by these groups. Instead of attempting to reach a definitive answer, I shall try to clarify the intricate and seemingly insoluble issues involved. In each instance I will suggest where Buddhism may be illuminative. For it does seem that we are living in an age of dis-solution and solutions seem to evade us. This should prompt us to investigate further than the customary Western panaceas. Some of the present remedies are too simplistic and posed as extremist choices: e.g., one option described by

some ecologists is a mystic dissolution into a state of benign, yet
ineffectual, assimilation with all of reality. In contrast, the dissolution
proposed by more extreme readings of deconstruction implies that,
because meaning is indeterminable, one is incapable of constructive
commitment to any change. These exclusive, yet ultimately quietistic
positions should motivate us to question a system that can only think in
terms of diametric opposites, leading finally to the reaction that all is
either infinite stasis or an endless replay of irresolution.

It is of course difficult to specify a particular Buddhist response to
our Western dilemma, given the complexity and the variant readings of
the different schools of Buddhist thought. I will choose relatively
straightforward examples that are common to both Theravāda and
Mahāyāna traditions, and eschew involvement with different
interpretations that are not relevant to the immediate purpose of this
paper.

ECOLOGICAL ALTERNATIVES

The strategic combination of feminism and ecology with its
commitment to altering the current world-view is a potent combination.
The resultant hybrid of ecofeminism, however, is not an immediately
compelling one.[4] Their common platform at times seems to have a
manufactured feel to it—as if hastily patched together to rebut the
prevailing Western severance between civilization and nature. Yet their
mutual concern to restore a balanced relationship between humanity and
nature, to "heal the wounds" wrought by a dichotomizing mind-set,
does have a persuasive rhetorical force. The question remains whether
the solutions proposed with regard to both women and nature are an
adequate, let alone effective, means of achieving this goal.

Virtually all the women who write in the area of ecofeminism agree
with postmodern feminists on the cause that is at the root of the
domination both of women and of nature (though they do not see the
those forms of exploitation as absolutely identical). Kay Warren
succinctly presents this view:

---

[4] The term "ecofeminism" is attributed to a Frenchwoman, Françoise d'Eaubonne, in
her *Le féminisme ou la mort* (Paris: Pierre Horay, 1974) 213-52. The literature on the
topic is vast. See especially the journals *Environmental Ethics* and *Philosophy East and
West* which in the last decade have published a variety of articles by both men and
women on topics concerned with ecology, ethics, feminism and Buddhism.

ecological feminism is the position that there are important connections—
historical, experiential, symbolic, theoretical—between the domination of
women and the domination of nature, an understanding of which is crucial
to both feminism and environmental ethics.[5]

From a feminist perspective, the above systems of oppression
derive from the prevailing philosophical orientation of the Western
world.[6] The basic mode of binary structures reinforces a pattern of
inclusion and exclusion, whereby an alternate (and inferior) modality is
denigrated or suppressed. In combination with the alleged endemic
androcentric bias of Western culture, which accepts the male as norm, it
inculcates a patriarchal social system encoding a hierarchy of
participants. The dominant self is also identified with male and public
norms. Intrinsic to this orientation is a sharp bifurcation between the
intellectual and physical worlds. Insofar as this dispensation makes man
the measure of all things, "Humanity is defined oppositionally to both
nature and the feminine."[7]

Many ecofeminists are critical of certain developments within the
environmental movement, such as that of deep ecology. This is because
deep ecology (e.g., as presented in the work of Arne Naess[8]), while
intensely committed to restoring a right relationship to nature, remains
ignorant of the equally urgent feminist agenda of restoring a right
relationship with women. A more comprehensive platform is then
promoted. Certain feminists of a psychological reconstructionist
persuasion tend to favor the adoption of "feminine" categories. Often
this option is tied to a revalorization of the goddess or a female principle.
The processes of nature are idealized and a goddess-worshipping

[5] Karen J. Warren, "The Power and the Promise of Ecological Feminism,"
Environmental Ethics 12 (Summer, 1990), 126.

[6] Both Western idealism and realism and their inevitably exclusionary binarism have
operated in such a way that, whatever was the acceptable model of rationality,
women were deemed deficient. Genevieve Lloyd documents this well in *The Man of
Reason* (Minneapolis, Minn.: University of Minnesota Press, 1994). Also see Carolyn
Merchant, *The Death of Nature: Women, Ecology and the Scientific Revolution* (San
Francisco, Calif.: Harper, 1983).

[7] Val Plumwood, "Nature, Self, and Gender: Feminism, Environmental Philosophy
and the Critique of Rationalism," *Hypatia* 6 (Spring 1991), 11.

[8] Arne Naess, *Ecology, Community and Lifestyle: A Philosophical Approach* (Oslo,
Norway: Oslo University Press, 1977). For a feminist response see Marti Kheel,
"Ecofeminism and Deep Ecology: Reflections on Identity and Difference," in
Reweaving the World, eds. Irene Diamond and Gloria Feman Orenstein (San Francisco,
Calif.: Sierra), 128-137.

community is evoked as providing a model for all the requisite changes in consciousness and conduct. "Peaceful and progressive societies thrived for millennia where gynocentric values prevailed.... In short we have lived sanely before, we can do it again."[9]

Although some more rationally inclined revisionists are not as enthusiastic in advocating such goddess-identified or gynocentric attributes, they nonetheless argue in favor of "feminine" qualities. They endorse these while recognizing that such values are relative and not innate to women, and that women's seeming closeness to nature is actually a construct and a result of patriarchal designations. The affinity of women and nature need no longer bear the brunt of negative connotations. Ariel Salleh exemplifies this view when she states: "[E]cofeminism, specifically, is about a transvaluation of values, such that the repressed feminine, nurturant side of our culture can be woven into all social institutions and practices."[10]

In contrast, social reformist feminists gravitate to a more materialist analysis. In her critique of the psychological position, Janet Biehl worries that embracing traditional "feminine" attitudes, whether from an essentialist or constructivist stance, only serves to reinforce stereotypes. "Sexist characterizations like 'intuitive,' 'irrational,' 'hysterical,' and 'unpredictable' have been slapped on women for centuries. At the very least, this should warn women about reckless use of metaphors in trying to form an ecofeminist ethics."[11] Biehl advocates instead a participatory democratic society which focuses its attention on decentralized and local groups. Such co-operative collectives will undermine the hegemony of capitalist society politics through their populist appeal.[12] Her argument is that the qualities ecofeminists tend to associate solely with female interests are, in fact, subjects of vital concern to men as well as women.

What Biehl seems particularly troubled about is the fact that a holistic vision, if left open-ended, can all too easily degenerate into a narcissistic identification with all life in a way which removes all grounds for decisions of value. This results in simplistic expressions that proclaim we are part of an inseparable bond with the cosmos and all

---

[9] Charlene Spretnak, "Toward an Ecofeminist Spirituality," in *Healing the Wounds*, ed. Judith Plant, (Philadelphia, Penn.: New Society Publishers, 1989), 131.

[10] Ariel Salleh, "The Ecofeminism/Deep Ecology Debate: A Reply to Patriarchal Reason," *Environmental Ethics* 14/3 (Fall, 1992), 203.

[11] Janet Biehl, *Finding Our Way: Rethinking Ecofeminist Politics* (Montreal: Black Rose Books, 1991), 24.

[12] Ibid., 151-153.

other living creatures, and that just by realizing this, balance and harmony can be restored. This realization is often extolled as uniquely "feminine." Such expressions betray a romanticization of nature and relationship in a way that belies the fact that nature is not always benign, that relationships are not always supportive, and that women themselves are not naturally nurturant.[13] Such a participatory mysticism tends to absolve all difference (not just opposition) and often neglects to focus on elements that need a discerning eye to call attention to the potential disruptive, if not harmful aspects of relationship. The question of relationship, then, is a crucial one in the light of the rejection of the individualistic version of a self.

The issue seems to be one where a transmutation rather than a reclamation of gender-linked values is needed. Yet it would also appear that the whole system of binary logic, with its relegation of all that pertains to women as subordinate, requires revision. The need is for a world where neither "masculine" or "feminine" qualities are sex-specific and where neither is valorized over the other, rather than a revalorization of "feminine" attributes. For while connectedness and empathy may be necessary to limit domination tendencies, they should not erase rational and analytical skills. Ultimately, it would seem to be a question of the way in which a person exercises all these skills and capacities in a culture that promotes the balanced contributions of both aspects. The final proviso, however, would be that such qualities should always be appreciated within a framework of knowing and being where acquisitive or exploitative behavior is no longer encouraged. Conjunctive rather than disjunctive modes of interaction are also in order.

Thus, while ecofeminism provides a powerful diagnosis of the problem, most of the solutions offered have suffered from being parasitic on the system they criticize and thus perpetuate a counter binarism. The question that becomes crucial in the wake of the dismissal of the monolithic view of self is the definition of identity that is now to be

---

[13] Perhaps Charlene Spretnak's *States of Grace* (San Francisco, Calif.: Harper, 1991) is an example of a well-intentioned work that skirts these issues. She develops the idea of what she terms "ecological postmodernism". Integral to this movement is the experience of graced consciousness. Such a state is beyond our usual fragmented and dualistic consciousness. As such, it is described as the purview of mystics, poets and creative beings from all ages and religions. This optimistic and open-minded approach oversimplifies the divergences in these various allegiances (and ignores that they have often been elitist). It also ignores the fact that they have promoted forms of mind-body dualism that are not easily reconciled with the life-affirming and holistic vision of mind and body, nature and spirit, promoted by ecofeminism.

associated with women and nature. Inevitable questions follow: Before any vision of unity or collective identity, do women, as excluded others, first need to come into their own? Or should they reject, for the sake of ecological survival, any compensatory claims for acquiring individuality (identified with an assertive self)? This seems particularly significant for women, for if they opt for a unitive model they could become taken for granted again, or dissolved in an amorphous (yet male-identified) conglomerate. What would seem to be more appropriate is a structure of relations which, while it no longer subscribes to oppositional or hierarchical modalities, also does not succumb either to the amorphousness of interminable displacement, or to a facile harmonious fusion.

Perhaps this is where Buddhism could be instructive, due to the implications of its "middle way." As often stated, these insights represent neither a nihilistic nor determinist description of reality, but a radical interrogation of the assumed self-sufficient status of any entity— be it a person or an object. At the same time, these teachings are vital components of a Buddhist world-view that avoids dyadic contrasts by emphasizing the mutual interdependency of all entities. And despite the many and varied schools that have proliferated under the name of Buddhism, there is one tenet that appears central to all of them. As Leslie Kawamura describes it: "the term Buddhism refers to a perceptual process 'of seeing' (darśana), a seeing in which concepts do not impede one's perception of reality as-it-is."[14] This intuitive insight into the nature of reality, unadorned by the metaphysical trappings of an essentialist nature, is accepted as the experience that constituted the Buddha's enlightenment. Although different accounts emphasize distinct elements of this experience, and although, as G. C. Pande observes, present-day evaluation of both its origin and significance differ, all schools agree that the one vital aspect of reality as-it-is as understood by the Buddha is the principle of *pratītya samutpāda*, variously translated as: dependent co-arising, mutually dependent causation, dependent origination, conditioned co-production or genesis.[15] The Buddha wanted to break us

---

[14] Leslie Kawamura, "Principles of Buddhism," *Zygon*, 25/1 (March, 1990), 59.

[15] For a brief survey in the Theravāda tradition see Govind Chandra Pande, *Studies in the Origins of Buddhism* (Delhi: Motilal Banarsidass, [1957] 1983); David Kalupahana also surveys the pre-Mādhyamika developments in the Pāli Nikāyas in *Causality: The Central Philosophy of Buddhism* (Honolulu: University of Hawaii Press, 1975); Frederick J. Streng discusses the Mādhyamika elaboration of *śūnyatā* on the theme of *pratītya samutpāda* in *Emptiness: A Study in Religious Meaning* (Nashville, Tenn.: Abingdon, 1967).

of our bad habits of perceiving ourselves as unconditioned and independent, for otherwise we would continue indefinitely in our self-inflicted cycle of delusion and dis-ease. But the corrective disposition is not to be achieved by will-power (in the Western sense), nor by a change in intellectual ideology. The Buddha himself described this conversion as going against the grain of accustomed physical and mental comportment to discern something that is complex, subtle and above all elusive.

But how is one to cleanse the doors of perception? A long and painstaking discipline of mind and body was the requisite program— involving both exacting physical watchfulness and acute introspective alertness—tempered by compassion, not rigidity. With such exquisite attention to detail, mindfulness (*sati*) gradually leads to awakening. When one sees reality—the "suchness" of things—unimpeded by desires to possess or manipulate, there is no longer a compulsion to organize the world according to any preordained categories. Along with insight comes not only non-attachment but an unqualified concern (*karunā*) for all sentient beings. Freed from attachment, we no longer want or require reason to provide solace and security, and no longer do we construct edifices of intellectual ingenuity that are inherently incapable of meeting our overinflated expectations. And, as Western ecologists intuit, no longer do we regard it as our God-given imperative to divide and conquer.

This reorganization of our perceptual apparatus and demeanor is salutary for appreciating the immediacy of each interaction with our environment, which is no longer apprehended as divisible into separate units. As Kenneth Inada observes:

> In order to stop this wanton depletion and destruction, we must have a new understanding and, most importantly, a new vision of things. Here the original insight of the historical Buddha could come into play. Rather than taking off on some metaphysical flight to explain experience, the Buddha concentrated on man's [sic] experiential nature and came up with a startling insight: a vision of the open unity, clarity, and continuity of existence. To involve man's nature is, then, to involve at once his more extensive and unlimited relationship to his surroundings. In other words, man is not alone but thoroughly relational, and the grounds for a relational nature must be found within man's own nature and not in something external, to which he must react on a one-to-one basis.[16]

---

[16] Kenneth Inada, "Environmental Problematics in the Buddhist Context," *Philosophy East and West*, 37/2 (April, 1987), 146.

One scholar who has done much to connect these ideas of Buddhism and ecology, while formulating a revised notion of self, is Joanna Macy. In a recent article she discusses the need for the dismantling of the traditional egocentric construct of the self in order to allow the emergence of what she terms the "ecological self or the eco-self, co-extensive with other beings and the life of our planet."[17] When this happens, one ceases to adhere to the type of pathological individualism that Macy believes characterizes our contemporary civilization. In its place there appears an awareness that Macy describes as the "greening of the self." As a result, an understanding comes that "[w]e are profoundly interconnected and therefore we are all able to recognize and act upon our deep, intricate, and intimate inter-existence with each and every other being. That true nature of ours is already present in our pain for the world."[18]

She expands on this version of *pratītya samutpāda* in her book *The Dharma of Natural Systems*, where she undertakes a mutual hermeneutic exercise between *pratītya samutpāda* and general systems theory, finding in them similar accounts of an interdependent mode of causation.[19] Macy's claim is that both models offer the needed revolution in the thought patterns by which we view reality, a revolution which requires to be put into practice if we are to save our world from ecological disaster. Implicit in both forms is a revised understanding of the notion of causality. "Mutual causality, as both Buddhist teachings and general systems theory attest, involves the perception that the subject of thought and action is in actuality a dynamic pattern of activity interacting with its environment and inseparable from experience."[20]

To act in these circumstances is, for Macy, to be aware of the reciprocal repercussions of any thought or deed. Actions are no longer future goal-oriented, and instrumentalist reasoning gives place to a profound sense of responsibility. This is not the culpability of guilt, but a

---

[17] Joanna Macy, "The Greening of the Self," *Dharma Gaia*, ed. Allan Hunt Badiner (Berkeley, Calif.: Parallax Press, 1990) 53.

[18] Ibid., 61.

[19] In this article I confine myself to Macy's use of the Theravada view of *pratītya samutpāda* and do not explore the later variations of ßunyata in the work of Nagajuna and Hua-yen Buddhism. For further refinements see Francis H. Cook, *Hua-yen Buddhism: The Jewel Net of Indra* (University Park, Penn.: Pennsylvania University Press, 1977) and David Loy, "Indra's Postmodern Net," *Philosophy East and West*, 43/3 (July, 1993), 481-510.

[20] Joanna Macy, *The Dharma of Natural Systems: Mutual Causality in Buddhism and General Systems Theory* (Albany, NY: State University of New York Press, 1991), 114.

recognition of our mutual involvement in an intricate network that supports the efficacy of actions, motivated by non-attachment and loving-kindness, to change karmic structures. The notion of identity involved is not one of autonomy or negativity, but one that is constantly formed and reformed by the ceaseless interaction of inherent elements. As Macy observes, "we are, quite literally, part of each other—free neither from indebtedness to our fellow-beings nor responsibility for them."[21] In this model there is evident a new perspective that could inform our contemporary deliberations, without resorting either to a mystical oneness without practical implications, or to a hydra-headed many-ness without resolution.

REFORMATTING THE SELF

The definition of the idea of "self" has been a problematic one for Western feminists. How is one to allow for a sense of personal integrity and independence, qualities that Western women have been deprived of by philosophical/theological prescriptions as well as cultural mores, without imitating the discredited autocratic mode of individuality that has been the norm for Western males? One of the more creative alternatives has been explored by Catherine Keller. Inspired by process theology, her *From a Broken Web* takes a novel approach to definitions of self and otherness.[22] Influenced primarily by Alfred North Whitehead and John Cobb, Keller strives to displace the accustomed self-identical ideal, with its modes of separation and distinction, in favor of a more interrelated and pluralistic model.[23] This is a difficult agenda, and the weaknesses obvious in Keller's project are similar to those of the process model itself, particularly the problem of balancing the increasing complexity of its evolving components within a projected harmonious whole. Keller, however, endeavors to bring a unique perspective by arguing that the process model's interconnected strategy and its incorporation of otherness is particularly pertinent for women. This is because, in its solution, process thought avoids the extremes of

---

[21] Ibid., 194.

[22] Catherine Keller, *From a Broken Web* (Boston, Mass.: Beacon, 1986).

[23] The work of Alfred North Whitehead, (especially *Religion in the Making* [London: Macmillan, 1926]) has had a major influence on Christian theology (as in the works of Charles Hartshorne, *The Divine Relativity: A Social Conception of God* [New Haven, Conn.: Yale University Press, 1948] and John B. Cobb and David Ray Griffin, *Process Theology: an Introductory Exposition* [Philadelphia, Penn.: Westminster Press, 1976]).

separatism or solubility (as Keller terms them) that have pervaded Western notions of the self.

Keller's vision is posed in terms of what it means for a woman today to have a self. To describe a self that is neither separate nor submerged, Keller seeks to articulate a connected self that incorporates both a one-ness in many-ness and a many-ness in one-ness—i.e., a self that is connected but not indistinguishable, different yet not separate. It is an intricate and exacting procedure—one that flies in the face of traditional logic—and to achieve it Keller has to forego the consolations of traditional substance metaphysics. Hence the use of Whitehead's process thought where the model is one of continuous creation. For how can one be distinct yet related, related but not fused or identified, except as part of a process that relinquishes the need to distinguish in order to to achieve a higher unity? This constant expansiveness, minus any imposed disjunction, is interpreted in process theology as God at work in the world. Thus otherness, as a category of exclusion or discrimination, has no place in process thought. Many-ness, formerly assigned to the province of otherness and difference by metaphysical distinctions, is now accepted as a given rather than viewed as an obstacle to be overcome. Any differentiation that occurs depends instead on the capacity of the multiplicity already present to enhance its freedom by further diversification. Ideally, in Whitehead's schema, this diversification is simultaneously a move in the direction of greater harmony and simplicity. God is both many and one, and thus any increase is both an intensification of a coextensive unity *and* plurality.

With specific reference to women, Keller posits that such interconnectedness allows women to expand their own boundaries while maintaining an inherent connectivity. This model of relatedness, because of its constant extension and exploration, does not endorse any stereotypical definition or idealization of femininity. The concept of femininity, as well as that of a self, is always subject to change and revision. Again, it is the process notion of God as *becoming*, rather than of *Being* or of any permanent essence, that is recommended as the mark of women. Thus there is no longer any underlying unitive self. Instead, each moment or occasion in the process of intensification is constitutive of a self. "Self" as a term becomes diversified. Our identity is made up of multiple occurrences, each of which constitutes a self. As a result, what Keller terms a "person" is a composite of these selves or occasions. In adopting this understanding of the term "person" Keller is striving to avoid the snares of substantive versions of the self in favor of a more mobile and associative one. What she strives to maintain is that one can persist in remaining the same person, as in forms of constancy despite change (as in a promise or a commitment), but this does not necessarily entail an identical subject, with an invariable reduplication of qualitative or quantitative attributes. "For 'person,' or 'personal order' (which Whitehead prefers, in order to avoid the emphasis on human consciousness), describes the way individual self events are bonded together to produce the sense of continuity we feel—more or less—from childhood to death."[24] Keller follows Whitehead in using the term "soul" as a synonym for this appreciation of a dynamic whole, comprised of many selves or occasions. "*Soul* is another word Whitehead uses interchangeably with person, to indicate this intermingling continuity between our moments...Soul, or person, is the society composed of the stream of selves."[25]

Keller contrasts this construct of interrelated selves with the two types of self-description that she views as having been regulative in the Western heritage. These are those of the separative self (distinctive of men) and the soluble self (characteristic of women). Whereas the separative self demarcates mastery and possession, the soluble self defers to prescribed norms. The soluble self describes women's tendencies to please or remain dependent in ways that prevented their acquisition of self-determination or self-respect. Neither of these defective identities is in accord with the process ideal of continuous creation, for they promote inflexible stereotypes. Keller wants to replace such restrictive classifications with a connected form of the self (or rather selves) that resonates with the pluralist and non-oppositional capacities of process thought. Nonetheless, Keller is only too aware of the quandary involved for women in maintaining the integrity of this interwoven model as distinct from the more conventional female tendency to merger and absorption. So she emphasizes the shifting and fluctuating modality of selves—where change and creativity are basic to any definition of a person—as distinct from customary static and normative definitions of the self. A woman's God-given task is to realize her identity within this flow of energies. This interconnection, Keller believes, is best portrayed by the image of a web—a filigree of networks, tracing the coalescing and diverging movements of the person and her surroundings.[26]

---

[24] Keller, 195-196.
[25] Ibid., 196.
[26] Ibid., 223- 228.

Keller's depiction of the evolving perception of multiple selves need not be specific to women (though at this time it is perhaps strategically important for women to mark their difference). Whereas continuity through time can be considered as the mark of a domineering mode of autonomy and control, the fluidity and flexibility that are indicative of the process modality put all substantialist versions of similarity as repetition into perpetual question. The model of process thought is thus a remedy for any system, patriarchal or otherwise, that has rigidified or hypotasized sameness in opposition to difference. The new model perceives identity as emergent within the matrix of a creative transformation. It relocates the notion of divinity as inherent in the process itself. This marks a return to the Biblical ideal of God as active in the world, as present in the midst of events, as well as a recognition of human beings as co-creators. Dominance and control are absent. The paradigm fostered is that of human flourishing, of witnessing the in-born divine impulse to create co-operatively. God is now recognized as inherent in the process itself.

But what of the objection sometimes raised to process thought, that what it does is virtually eliminate otherness in the name of a monistic whole? Keller, like Whitehead, is adamant that any totality in this system is essentially plural; there is no symbiotic union of a dependent kind. There can be *one* only in and through the many *ones* that comprise it.

> But Whitehead refuses any monistic One: for him (indeed as for Leibniz) the universe as a totality is essentially plural. It becomes one only in each of the many *ones*, the complex compositions of feeling that are the actual entities. Internal relatedness means that everything in some sense is *really* part of me, however dimly felt.[27]

Nonetheless, when relatedness is talked of in such a context, as consisting in my being part of everything and everything being part of me, the boundaries begin to blur. As a result, although it is fine for Keller to talk of the need for boundaries of the self that are more permeable and diffuse, the exact mode of the interrelationship and interconnection involved between the various parts and the whole becomes equivocal. And, while it must be acknowledged that Keller's attempt to define a novel conception of personal identity—one which can affirm itself without obliterating the other—is a genuine beginning in the search for new ways of identity and relationship, there nonetheless remains the

---

[27] Ibid., 184.

danger of dissolution. Keller herself is alert to this dilemma and advocates a method of "ambivalence" for the movement beyond the traditional self-sufficient ego to a connected self. For the task now is to avoid both the conventional female-identified pitfall of dissolution as well as the new deconstructive dispersion of any pretensions to autonomous identity (associated with erstwhile male privilege). At this stage, the best that Keller can offer is the observation that the relational fluidity she seeks (that can hold fast under such pressures).

> has everything to do with staying conscious of body, of all the flux of emotion felt in the body; and with staying conscious of the ebb and flow of influences from others, the different ones, the ones making up a particular world. Such consciousness-raising lifts up the politics of a self-in-relation, which becomes a self-creating community.[28]

Anne Klein, in a comparative analysis of Western and Buddhist notions of the self, offers an astute commentary on the problematic encountered by Keller's work in trying to negotiate between the separative and soluble modes. According to Klein, the difficulty arises because many Westerners, particularly women, find themselves in a predicament when they attempt to integrate a psychology of relatedness with a unitive ontology. Buddhist analysis, which does not approach epistemology and ontology in the same reified and dichotomous way, could help Westerners to appreciate this incongruity and provide a more appropriate understanding of selfhood. Central to Klein's focus is her own emphasis on awareness of how we constitute self-definitions in accordance with often conflicting structures of meaning. To recognize this is to be no longer at the mercy of their divisive and estranging interests.[29] A definition of self proposed in these conditions mirrors the changing patterns of our existence rather than attempts to control proceedings.[30]

---

[28] Catherine Keller, "'To Illuminate Your Trace': Self in Late Modern Feminist Theology," *Listening*, 25/3 (1990), 222.

[29] Anne Carolyn Klein, "Finding a Self: Buddhist and Feminist Perspectives," *Shaping New Visions: Gender and Values in American Culture* (Ann Arbor, Mich.: UMI Research, 1987), 191-218.

[30] As Steven Collins (*Selfless Persons: Imagery and Thought in Theravāda Buddhism*, [Cambridge: Cambridge University Press, 1982],110) demonstrates in his discussion of *pratītya samutpāda* (as the fourth argument in support of *anātman*), any attribution of permanence as endowing the self or person is replaced by "the idea of a congeries of impersonal, conditioned elements." The complexity and multiplicity of a self now appear as interlinked moments where events occur synchronously rather than in

In her recent book *The Great Bliss Queen*, influenced by the teachings of the Geluk order of Tibetan Buddhism of selflessness as emptiness (*śūnyatā*), Klein makes the point succinctly for a Western audience: "The self negated in the theory and practice of selflessness is synonymous, not with persons in general, but with a person regarded, however subtly, as independent from the mind and body that is its basis. No such self exists." She continues, to reassure those who equate Buddhism with the denial of any sort of personal integrity or identity: "The self so vigorously denied in Buddhist philosophy must not be confused with an integrated sense of self-worth, which neither modern psychology nor Buddhist traditions...would urge one to discard."[31] Klein also stresses that Buddhism also does not wish to impart a sense of helplessness, or an evasion of responsibility such as that associated with the soluble self that Keller sees as a predominantly feminine characteristic in the West. For Klein, "[b]oth Buddhists and feminists would agree that self-abandoning behavior is wasteful, and Buddhists would further emphasize that it fails to get at the ontological root of the issue."[32] So what is the ontological root of the issue?

Klein formulates her response with reference both to feminism and to those theorists who are attracted to the destabilizing strategies of postmodernism. Klein explains:

> From a Buddhist perspective, the contemporary fascination with the incoherent and uncapturable multiplicities that construct self and knowledge suggests an intellectual history that never took sufficient note of the interdependent, constructed, and impermanent nature of things in the first place. Recognition of constructedness does not, for Buddhists, devalorize the unconstructed.[33]

This answer provides a diagnosis of Western consciousness that, because of the dualisms endemic to its metaphysics, can only conceive of essentialism and constructivism as irreconcilable. Yet it is here that an important distinction should be made, for while Buddhism cannot subscribe to any notion of essentialism in the Western sense, it does

---

specific sequential patterns. The world operates as a radically empirical system rather than as an ontological composite. On this point, though with varying interpretations, both Theravāda and Mahāyāna schools agree. See John Koller, *Oriental Philosophies* (New York: Charles Scribner's Sons, 1985), 165-175.

[31] Anne Carolyn Klein, *The Great Bliss Queen: Buddhists, Feminists, and the Art of the Self* (Boston, Mass.: Beacon, 1995), 130.

[32] Ibid., 131.

[33] Ibid., 140.

allow for the notion of an unconditioned which is, in fact, the actual experience of selflessness or emptiness. This perception, however, is not an intellectual definition but the experience of non-dualism inculcated by the practice of mindful meditation on one's conditioned existence. Thus, in Buddhism, the conditioned and unconditioned are not mutually exclusive. Klein elaborates on this co-existence, while contrasting it with the postmodern position:

> The stabilizing force of concentration balances the sense of destabilization that comes from undoing one's previous experience of the world. Buddhists would agree with postmodernists that the mind and its activities are linguistic in general, but not that mental functioning is irreducibly linguistic. Unlike the textual idolatry of some contemporary theory, the words that are the starting point for reflection on emptiness and compassion do not continue to govern the subject in the same way throughout the developmental process. The mind is not thought alone; nor is it separate from bodily energies. It is also clarity and knowing. And Buddhists emphasize that this clarity and knowing can experientially be fused with the unconditioned emptiness.[34]

Such a conscious method and its implications could be of assistance both to postmodern feminists and to Keller, who is striving to express not only the interweaving patterns of a personal thematics of identity but a more comprehensive interconnection with the paths of other women and men, and with the rhythms of life itself and the cosmos. Her interrelated self no longer needs to be in danger of being soluble, nor involved in a teleological process that posits a soul.

This observation regarding coexistence is also applicable to the stalemate that besets contemporary feminism, both in its dependence on theory and in its insistence on seeing essentialist and constructivist versions of feminism, and their respective theories of self and agency, as mutually exclusive. The West may be still too attached to its intellectual edifice and conceptual structures to be open to a Buddhist contribution, for Buddhism does entail a radical realignment of values. As Klein observes: "Like the cultivation of calm and concentration, the experience of emptiness entails a different order of interiority than the textual, content-laden localized and particularized subjectivity associated with contemporary theory and modern psychologizing."[35] Yet Klein's work has charted a path that offers new ways of reconsidering a sense of

---

[34] Ibid., 138.
[35] Ibid., 140.

selflessness beyond the bifurcations of Western consciousness and the damaging effects a monolithic system has wrought personally and systemically by its dualisms of body and soul, nature and culture.

POSTMODERN FOIBLES

What of the challenge attributed to postmodernism? Does it lead to nihilism, as some of its critics charge, or is there also a constructive agenda contained within its operations?[36] Whereas initially it would appear that deconstruction articulates insights similar to Buddhism regarding the patterning of events and the questioning of a metaphysical self, it cannot provide an alternative of stabilizing practice. As evidence of this, the a/theologian Mark C. Taylor, a disciple of Derrida's type of deconstruction, voices his impression of the much-elaborated demise of God and the concept of self in the wake of deconstructive displacement:

> The death of the transcendent Father need not be the complete disappearance as an immanent and eternal process of dialectical development. The death of solitary selfhood need not be the total disappearance of self, but it can be seen as the birth of universal selfhood in which each becomes itself by relation to all.[37]

Taylor implies that this exploration will involve a radical suspicion of fundamental philosophical and theological assumptions, but he gives no clue as to how any further comprehension is to be negotiated. Instead, he resorts to aphorisms about necessary fictions, about the inevitable possibility/impossibility conundrum that marks all conceptual formulations, and about the enigma of a transcendent/immanent God. He indulges in erratic word games, all contrived to illustrate that one must learn to live, even to exult in paradox.[38] But there is no indication as to how this knowledge is to be achieved or maintained. There is also no specification as to whether Taylor is discussing the being of God or

---

[36] Eve Tavor Bannet in *Structuralism and the Logic of Dissent* (Urbana, Ill.: University of Illinois Press, 1989) admits that Derrida's deconstruction, as a strategy of postmodernism, is indeed destructive, but of suitable targets: "What Derrida's rule set out to destroy is nothing less than the ethno-centrism and self-referentiality of the West: the 'mythology of the white man' who takes his own logos for the universal form of reason, and who transforms his own consciousness into a universal form of appropriation, who makes everything and everyone the 'same' as himself, and who makes himself the master of all things (and all beings)" (222).

[37] Mark C. Taylor, *Deconstructing Theology* (New York: Crossroad, 1982), 102.

[38] Ibid., 107-126.

simply the inability of human representations to capture a noumenal reality. There is, of course, a crucial difference. It is one thing to demonstrate the inadequacy of human efforts to secure an abiding absolute. Buddhism does as much. But it is quite another to dispute the existence of a divine principle simply because of the incommensurable levels of discourse involved. Buddhism wisely refrains from any definitive declarations regarding such ultimacy, regarding the careful cultivation of mindfulness a sufficient challenge to alleviate distress and doubt. But deconstruction offers no such solace, and it is for this reason that its reputation of nihilism arises. To dally in the interstices of human knowledge without guidance can court madness and desolation, for few are equipped to face such random occurrences. Far better, as in Buddhism, a simple practice which attends to the moment, which aids the management of unruly impulses in the direction of a more tolerable and tolerant conduct. In addition, however, there is the acceptance in Buddhism that non-conceptual intuition (as well as deepened compassion) is an integral part of this prescription. Deconstruction offers no such corrective and often flaunts only a superficial (if seductive) ingenuity. As David Loy observes: "Derrida shows only that language cannot grant access to any self-present meaning; his methodology cannot settle the question whether our experience of language and the so-called objective world is susceptible to a radical transformation."[39]

Thus, with regard to deconstruction, Buddhism illuminates both its lack of clarity and of responsibility which prevent its chain of signifiers from constituting anything other than an accidental collision of heterogeneous linguistic forces. As a result, while deconstruction can be of benefit in guarding against the inclination to reify (including ideas of the self), it has much to learn from a tradition such as Buddhism regarding the need for a committed practice. Changing one's mindset is not merely a theoretical option, for this can lead to either a dilettantish virtuosity or the impasse of indecision. Deconstruction is focused solely on the unreliability of language and the instability of concepts, but it does not pursue this insight with the rigorous introspection of Buddhism in order to to understand the basis of one's reliance on such an inconstant mechanism. Buddhism alone encourages us to change the very nature of our perception of the world by the constant practice of daily mindfulness.

---

[39] David Loy, "The Deconstruction of Buddhism," *Derrida and Negative Theology*, ed. Harold Coward and Toby Foshay (Albany, NY: State University of New York, 1992), 250.

Similarly, while the combination of feminism and postmodernism illustrates well its iconoclastic strategy, any pragmatic application is lacking. For this reason, it does not receive the support of all feminists. Susan Hekman, a proponent, outlines the principle area of convergence: "The focus of both feminist and postmodern critiques of the subject is to expose the privileging of the subject that is at the root of the modern existence."[40] Consequently "[a] postmodern approach to feminism thus calls for a total rejection of the epistemology that rests on the subject/object dualism. It also calls for an approach that eschews any notion of the essentially feminine or a universal feminine sexuality."[41]

Such a strategy, however, could easily backfire. First, because it seems to indulge in the very essentialism it claims to challenge when it identifies masculinity with rationality as the source of the dualistic mindset. Secondly, women can become reduced to ciphers in a theoretical game where the feminine identity becomes a ploy to incapacitate the binary movements presupposed in any logic of identity. It could culminate in a stalemate where all women can do is resist the present system with cryptic deployments rather than use their energy to change it and forge an identity. The alternative is to start a new system outside present rules and regulations, but apart from appeals to body-language and *le parler femme* (*womanspeak*) on the part of the French thinker Luce Irigaray[42], there is no clear indication of how the world could actually be changed—though Irigaray claims that her poetics constitutes a utopian politics of a new order.[43] As yet, the integration of identity politics with social and cultural politics remains one of charged debate within feminism.

One of the most articulate voices in this debate is the African-American scholar bell hooks, who refuses to be confined to theoretical

---

[40] Susan J. Hekman, *Gender and Knowledge: Elements of a Postmodern Feminism* [Boston, Mass.: Northeastern Press, 1990), 92.

[41] Ibid., 93.

[42] Luce Irigaray, *This Sex Which Is Not One*, trans. Catherine Porter (Ithaca, NY: Cornell University Press, 1985). Originally published as *Ce sexe qui n'est pas un* (Paris: Les Editions de Minuit, 1977).

[43] In a recent work *je, tu, nous* (New York: Routledge, 1993) Irigaray explores further her program of *"a theory of gender as sexed* and a rewriting of the rights and obligations of each sex, *qua different*, in social rights and obligations"(13). This seems a retrieval of a more modernist agenda, though Irigaray states this alone will lead to true equality. The problematic of defining the interrelationship of one sex with the other, where the identity of each is preserved and respected, is addressed in her work *An Ethics of Sexual Difference* (Ithaca, NY: Cornell University Press, 1995).

speculations. Her work is an exemplar of a committed lifestyle that reflects an ethos of awareness where theory and practice mutually inform each other. Interestingly, she has a positive though qualified attitude to postmodernism.

> Postmodern culture with its decentered subject can be the space where ties are severed or it can provide the occasion for new and varied forms of bonding. To some extent, ruptures, surfaces, contextuality, and a host of other happenings create gaps that make space for oppositional practices which no longer require intellectuals to be confined by narrow separate spheres with no meaningful connection to the world of everyday.[44]

Perhaps this approach is possible because hooks, who does not repudiate her Christian roots in a southern black community, has also been deeply influenced by Buddhism. Hooks' own practice acknowledges the intricate interweaving of questions of race, class and gender and an acknowledgement that women themselves are not immune to perpetuating structures of superiority, including a notion of a dominating self. She has been relentless in her criticism of the racism that has pervaded the feminist movement:

> Not only did white women act as if feminist ideology existed solely to serve their own interests...They were unwilling to acknowledge that non-white women were part of the collective group in American society. They urged black women to join "their" movement or in some cases the women's movement, but in dialogues and writings, their attitudes toward black women were both racist and sexist. Their racism did not assume the form of overt expressions of hatred; it was far more subtle. It took the form of simply ignoring the existence of black women or writing about them using common racist or sexist stereotypes.[45]

Hooks believes that resistance to such ingrained cultural deformation involves education which honors both the personal and the social dimensions, both theory and practice.[46] The white cultural hegemony that has operated to deny this honoring and respect must be addressed as it has brought about a society where "[b]lack people are

---

[44] bell hooks, "Postmodern Blackness," *Yearning: race, gender and cultural politics,* (Toronto: Between the Lines, 1992).
[45] bell hooks, *Ain't I A Woman: Black women and Feminism* (Boston, Mass.: South End Press, 1981), 137.
[46] bell hooks, "Educating Women: A Feminist Agenda," *Feminist Theory: From Margin to Center* (Boston, Mass.: South End Press, 1984), 112-115.

wounded in our hearts, minds, bodies and spirits."[47] Thus, most recently, she has devoted her energies to "healing the wounds" of the women of the African American community whose experiences of racism and abuse have led to self-destructive practices. Her principal focus is black women and their recuperation from the many forms of political and social oppression. Hooks terms this process "self- recovery" and invokes the words of the Vietnamese Buddhist monk Thich Nhat Hanh to support her vision.[48] Her practice, informed by compassion, seeks to center on discerning what form of activity is the most appropriate in any given circumstances (*upāya*).[49] In her analysis, hooks strives to articulate the intertwined nature of identity and community. She affirms that any formulation of identity is always interdependent with the complex ties that bind a community's self perception. This nonetheless involves being able to name, by mindful observation, not just instances of racism and sexism in the wider community, but the responsibility of each person to pay attention to his/her own failings. She does not exclude herself:

> To heal our wounds we must be able to critically examine our behavior and change. For years I was a sharp-tongued woman who often inappropriately lashed out. I have increasingly learned to distinguish between "reading" and truth-telling. Watching my behavior...helped me to change my behavior.[50]

Her discriminating practice thus does not preclude her undertaking an agenda of personal as well as social reform.[51] And it is from such a perspective that hooks does not allow others who follow a Buddhist path to recline in the complacency that following Buddhist practices such as mindfulness automatically frees a person from racism.

> Often white people share the assumption that simply following a Buddhist path means that they have let go of racism: coming out of radical movements—civil rights, war resistance—in the sixties and seventies, and going on to form Buddhist communities, they often see themselves as liberal

---

[47] Ibid., 11.
[48] bell hooks, "On Self-Recovery," *Talking Back : Thinking Feminist. Thinking Black* (Toronto: Between the Lines, 1988), 29-30.
[49] bell hooks, "The Joy of Reconciliation," *Sisters of the Yam: Black Women and Self-Recovery* (Toronto: Between the Lines, 1993), 169.
[50] bell hooks, *Sisters of the Yam*, 9.
[51] bell hooks, "Agent of change: An Interview with bell hooks," *Tricycle* 2/1 (Fall, 1992), 48-57.

and marginalized, proudly identifying with the oppressed. They are so attached to the image of themselves as non-racists that they refuse to see their own racism or the ways in which Buddhist communities may reflect racist hierarchies.[52]

Hooks talks of the questions she is asked regarding her teachers and her practice and the accompanying insinuations of superiority that cause her doubts regarding her worthiness and what it means to be a "real" Buddhist. These feelings are a legacy of oppression—the accustomed response of a disenfranchised community to assumptions of privilege that white society all too often unthinkingly and automatically appropriates.

> In those moments of contemplation and quiet, the awareness surfaces that so many people of color fear not being worthy in ways that escape the attention of our white comrades. This fear of not being worthy is not always a response to the reality of subjugation. It also has to do with the practice of humility, not being presumptuous, not assuming rights, and/or the experience of being in awe. [53]

In hooks' estimation, it is this conscious or unconscious cultural arrogance that has led many black people to question whether it is possible to remain loyal to their roots and also be a Buddhist in North America. Has Buddhism become the prerogative of white people who in their Buddhist lifestyle still carry attitudes of their dominant culture and who have great difficulty in accepting that their training has not eradicated them? Hooks' rigorous and honest questioning probes a sensitive nerve which is also a summons to greater sensitivity to the roots of the psychological and social formation of what could be termed a "racist self." As hooks herself says, "It is a challenge only a profound spiritual practice can help us meet."[54] Her work is a reminder that Buddhism in and of itself is not *the* solution to the ills that beset Western individuals and society as it nears the end of this century, and that Buddhism needs careful and measured evaluation before it is adopted.

---

[52] bell hooks, "Waking up to Racism," *Tricycle*, 4/3 (Fall, 1994), 43.
[53] Ibid., 45.
[54] Ibid., 45.

STRATEGIC OBSERVATIONS

There are other issues that need consideration regarding the practice and institutional structures of Buddhism as it journeys to the west. One matter of compelling interest is the degree to which scholars should insist on precise, if not pristine interpretations of the tenets of Buddhism. This discussion arises in the context of musings such as those by Kenneth Inada that the current expansion of Buddhist ideas in the West is comparable to the revolution that took place in Buddhism with the rise of the Mahāyāna movement and its spread to China and Japan.[55] Ann Klein assesses the situation succinctly:

> Buddhist traditions are famous for their ability both to change the cultures they visit and to be altered by them. Yet when Buddhist thought and practices moved to Southeast asia, or to China and the Korea and Japan, or to Tibet, they were part of a larger process of cultural exchange that extended over centuries. Never until today has such a wealth and variety of Buddhist resources—texts, practices and living teachers—been made available in so short a period of time to populations who are at the same time so ignorant of the cultures from which these traditions come.[56]

Gerald Larsen also raises some intriguing questions concerning the present transplantation of Buddhist ideas to the West.[57] Larsen ponders about the efficacy today of expressions from any religion that are historically dependent and thus contingent if not archaic in certain respects. He encourages a revitalization of our thinking to provide a more adequate response to our unique contemporary situation of an imminent end to our life-sustaining environment. For Larsen, past religious solutions do not address this set of circumstances. From another perspective, Inada's reflections also function as a preemptive advisory against colonization of ideas from other cultures, a tendency only too evident in past Western incursions into foreign territories. Intellectual colonization can be just as devastating for all concerned as the usurpation of land. Another sensitive issue is the relationship between the traditional practices of lay Asian people now living in the West, and the quasi-monastic lifestyle of many of the new Western converts to

---

[55] Inada, "Environmental Problematics in a Buddhist Context," 137.

[56] Klein, *The Great Bliss Queen*, 195.

[57] Gerald Larsen, "'Conceptual Resources' in South Asian for 'environmental ethics,' or the fly is still alive and well in the bottle," *Philosophy East and West*, 37/2 (1987), 150-159.

Buddhism.[58] So how should the current vigorous syncretism be viewed? By what standards should its current synergistic impulses be judged? As yet, there are no clear-cut answers and the issue is an open-ended one.

Such an approach will also place in relief certain queries and qualifications asked of Buddhism by the West. Thus, before any unqualified endorsement of the benefits of a Buddhist program, it is prudent to listen to some of the cautions voiced by women practitioners of Buddhism.[59] For Buddhism has not been without fault in its attitudes and practices towards women. The issue is a particularly complex one that is receiving more attention as women in the West follow Buddhist precepts and study the scriptures. The Pāli tradition maintains that, despite initial misgivings, the Buddha admitted women to monastic status as nuns and allowed that they could attain enlightenment. Yet this egalitarian impulse soon faded. It was supplanted by the prevailing cultural disregard for women. To support this, there are certainly disparaging references to women in the Pāli texts, such as the *Anguttara Nikāyas*, that I. B. Horner, for one, regards as later interpolations.[60] Women's sexuality has been regarded with particular suspicion if not, in some texts, in an extremely negative way.[61] With rare exceptions, women themselves have not been accorded the same spiritual recognition as men. As Anne Klein observes:

> Women in the West...are dealing not only with a tradition from another culture, one that was for much of its history primarily directed at men, but also with meditation practices and philosophical reflections—especially in the case of a Theravada and much Tibetan Buddhism—that were once the province of those who devoted their entire lives to them.[62]

In this area there still remains a discrepancy in Buddhism between theory and practice. This raises difficult questions regarding the

---

[58] Charles S. Prebish, *American Buddhism* (North Scituate Mass.: Duxbury Press, 1979).

[59] Rita Falk, "The Case of the Disappearing Nuns," *Unspoken Worlds: Women's Religious Lives* (Belmont, Calif.: Wadsworth, 1989), 155-165; Rita Gross, *Buddhism After Patriarchy* (Albany, NY: State University of New York Press, 1992).

[60] I. B. Horner, *Women Under Primitive Buddhism* (London: George Routledge & Sons Ltd., 1930), 105.

[61] Eva Neumaier-Dargyay, "Buddhist Thought from a Feminist Perspective," in *Gender, Genre and Religion*, eds. Morny Joy and Eva Neumaier-Dargyay (Waterloo, Ontario: Wilfrid Laurier Press, 1995), 145-70.

[62] Klein, *The Great Bliss Queen*, 65.

treatment of women in certain Buddhist countries,[63] though reform is already happening in the West where many women are becoming teachers and taking leadership roles in Buddhist communities.[64] The impact of such changes is difficult to predict at this time, but the fact that western women in large numbers are becoming Buddhist nuns and practitioners does present a distinct challenge to habitual custom and opinion. Anne Klein does not advocate an unconditional importation of Buddhist ideas, either. Her work is more concerned with exploring conceptual attitudes that could prove helpful: "I am not suggesting that Buddhist principles or practices be adopted wholesale by modern feminists or anyone else. I am, however, suggesting that the basic categories on which these practices and theories are premised can be helpful to contemporary women and to feminist theory."[65]

And perhaps, at this stage, that is the best summation of this whole exploration—suggestions for revision of the Western orientation which in itself seems incapable of the shift needed in both attitude and practice to alleviate its woes.

CONCLUSION

This has been an investigation of some of the interventions that are currently being proposed—mainly within religious settings (though not without secular ramifications)—as enabling the type of transformed consciousness (including a revised understanding of identity of the self) required to deal with our late twentieth-century predicament. In evaluating the merits and disadvantages of these diverse Buddhist interventions, it has become obvious that Buddhism cannot, of itself, supply all the answers.

Yet Buddhism does have much to offer a technologically dominated society, which often equates the mere verbalization of the factors in a problematic situation with an instant solution to it. In contrast, Buddhism eschews arid theorizing in the name of commitment to awareness of the internal and external barriers which cause estrangement in its many guises. It is only from insight into the

---

[63] For example, the massively organized sex trade in Thailand, which involves not only women. This is eloquently discussed by Chatsumarn Kabilsingh in her book *Thai Women in Buddhism* (Berkeley: Parallax Press, 1991), 67-86.

[64] Lenore Friedman, *Meetings with Remarkable Women: Buddhist Teachers in America*, (Boston, Mass.: Shambala, 1987).

[65] Klein, *The Great Bliss Queen*, 204.

mechanism of these operations, personal or political (or both), that a theory adequate to the circumstances can arise. Perhaps a realistic assessment of Buddhism's complex yet extraordinarily rich background can teach us that nostalgia for past ideals cannot rescue us, nor can elegant but empty improvisations that merely put the past into question. What is needed is a new way of relating to the world: a different sense of self. This would be a version that both critiques and constructs its practice with insights born of self-questioning honesty, i.e., by a mindfulness of our selves, in whatever guise they are manifested.

Buddhism does not attempt to provide logical proofs for such a sense of self but rather seeks to foster an intuition regarding the nature of the incongruity and diversity of experience. It teaches a disposition of non-attachment toward any ultimate solution. In this context, non-attachment should also be regarded as a manner of experience, rather than the suspension of all experience. Perhaps what the West needs to learn from Buddhism is this discriminating outlook rather than any specific theory, i.e., to forego its metaphysical predilections which tend to support one polarity at the expense of the other, and tend to sustain a managerial sense of self that orchestrates life. It could be that a tolerance of multiplicity and paradox is what we need to cultivate, but not in the manner of deconstructive dissolution. Instead, we need to live in a way that recognizes an experiential manifold which both converges and diverges. Unfortunately, given the West's philosophical and theological partiality for dualist frameworks, and for single-minded obsession with self-sufficiency, such a shift in consciousness may be a long time coming, despite these intimations. Nonetheless, a grafting of Buddhism is taking place in myriad fashions. Determining which hybrids will come to flourish would be a difficult and inconclusive exercise—and perhaps not a particularly Buddhist concern.

In No Wise is Healing Holistic

A DECONSTRUCTIVE ALTERNATIVE TO MASAO ABE'S
"KENOTIC GOD AND DYNAMIC SUNYATA"

ROBERT MAGLIOLA
ABAC UNIVERSITY, THAILAND

Masao Abe's keynote essay in *The Emptying God*[1] (1990) broaches a Buddhist contribution to Christian theology, and—both in its own right and in the Christian responses that follow—it initiates a new and important meeting between the notions of Buddhist emptiness and Christian *kenōsis* (Gk. 'emptying out'). In particular the workings of sameness and difference within Christianity's Triune God and between this God and the world are reexamined, in Abe's case with an eye towards showing that God and *śūnyatā* both function in a paradoxical way: namely—God/*śūnyatā* is not God/*śūnyatā*, and precisely because God/*śūnyatā* is not affirmative of itself, God/*śūnyatā* is truly God/*śūnyatā*.[2] Arguing that Abe's paradox, like all proper paradox, is holistic, I maintain that both *śūnyatā* and the Christian God are better limned by 'pure negative reference', a trace-concept that frequents Jacques Derrida's deconstructions.

Because pure negative references are constitutive of samenesses (i.e., *appoint*, *raise up* samenesses), healing—like all samenesses—is constituted precisely by differences (and not the 'other way around' as in the usual

---

[1] Masao Abe, "Kenotic God and Dynamic Sunyata," in *The Emptying God: A Buddhist-Jewish-Christian Conversation*, eds. John B. Cobb and Christopher Ives (Maryknoll, N.Y.: Orbis, 1990), 3–65.

[2] For example, see Abe, 15, 16, 33. I do not mean to imply that Abe equates the concepts of God and *śūnyatā*: rather, what he intends to compare (positively) is—as he sees it—their analogous operation of paradoxical negation and affirmation.

arguments, with differences established by a founding unity). Healing
works from bottom upwards, not from top downwards. Pure negative
differences are in non-paradoxical relation to the samenesses (they are
not, for example, interchangeable with the samenesses nor is it necessary
that their proportions match). The problematic of healing is radically at
stake here, of course, given that both in Buddhism and Christianity the
workings of sameness and difference engineer the world and arbitrate
the healing process. In this paper I broach 'pure negative reference' and
kindred maneuvers, first in their connection to Derrida and Buddhism,
and then by way of application to Trinitarian theology.

My *Derrida on the Mend*[3] (1984;86) proposes that—because of a
historical fluke or otherwise—Jacques Derrida's contemporary deconstruction of entitative metaphysics (logocentrism) happens to intersect
the Buddhist philosopher Nāgārjuna's (2nd century C.E.) programme of
deconstructing dharma-units. And the book traces the notion of
'devoidness' (that is, *śūnyatā* taken in its Nāgārjunist formulation[4])
within the tradition of Buddhism I call 'differential' (as opposed to the
Buddhist 'centric' or Absolutist tradition[5]). Masao Abe's thesis apropos
of 'emptying out' is paradoxical ("Sunyata is non-Sunyata," and vice
versa, and "therefore it is ultimate Sunyata"[6]). But, as Richard Robinson
rightly says, there are no paradoxes whatsoever in Nāgārjuna's

---

[3] Magliola, *Derrida on the Mend* (W. Lafayette: Purdue University Press, 1984;1986).

[4] I refer to the *śūnyatā* of Nāgārjuna's *Mūlamadhyamakakārikās*. This *śūnyatā* diverges
so much from the holistic *śūnyatā* of the Prajnaparamitan tradition (of which a
'Nāgārjuna' is also said to be a 'compiler') that many scholars—A. K. Warder being a
good case in point—posit more than one 'Nāgārjuna' or at least the fictional
attribution of his authorship to more than one tradition. There is also quite definitely
a much later pseudonymous Tantric 'Nāgārjuna', which complicates the history
further still. I give this matter more detailed treatment, at least insofar as it pertains to
the *Mūla-* and its *śūnyatā*, in a paper forthcoming in the Proceedings of the
Symposium on Buddhism and Modern Western Thought (Emmanuel College,
Cambridge University, July 3-5, 1992), ed. John Peacocke, Bolton Institute and
Manchester University.

[5] For definition of the Absolutist tradition and the opposing Madhyamikan one, see
B. K. Matilal, *Epistemology, Logic, and Grammar in Indian Philosophical Analysis* (Hague
and Paris: Mouton, 1971) 152-7, et passim; F. J. Streng, "Fundamentals of the Middle
Way," the appendix to his *Emptiness* (Nashville: Abingdon Press, 1967); Tarthang
Tulku, "A History of the Buddhist Dharma," in *Crystal Mirror* V (1977), pp. 98-101,
106-7; and Hsueh-Li Cheng, "Emptiness: Exoteric and Esoteric Buddhism," in *World
Sutric and Tantric Buddhist Conference Report* (Kaohsiung, Taiwan: Fo Kuang Press,
1988), 121-2.

[6] Abe, 27.

Mūlamadhyamakakārikās.[7] And paradox—as Derrida demonstrates[8]—is a logocentric formulation. Nor does it suffice, according to a radical point of view, to synthesize *śūnyatā* and image/concept (as some Buddhist schools do), so that 'empty image/concept' issues forth as the 'solution' (and the 'escape' from the fallacy of paradox). Such a solution, according to a radically deconstructive point of view, is simply too facile and neat:—it is a sleight-of-hand actually functioning to restore holism. Somehow, instead, the operation of images/concepts must be fractured, twisted, unsettled. Only the off-rational,[9] and not the rational or irrational, can frequent (i.e., *become*) devoidness.

As for Masao Abe's version of paradox, its binary of A = non-A is framed into a mystical oneness—the overall unity of this interchangeable opposition is congruent with itself. Even when Abe specifies we "should also put a cross mark 'X' on Sunyata, and render it Sun-X-yata,"[10] this is much more like the Heideggerian X than the deconstructive Derridean X.[11] Or, if you will, much more like the ineffable God of much Christian mysticism. And of course it is most like 'centric' Buddhism's unnameable, unobjectifiable 'ultimate *śūnyatā*'—beyond all concepts and images but taken to be a mystical totality. .

Masao Abe's Buddhism, as beautiful as it is, is thus a holistic Buddhism, and heals by way of holism: like most Japanese Zen, it operates broadly within the Svatantrikan-Madhyamikan-Yogacaric tradition. Not without reason has the Chinese Buddhologist, Hsueh-Li Cheng (University of Hawaii, Hilo), gone so far as to decry Japanese Zen's famous 'missionary to the West', D. T. Suzuki, as a 'transcendentalist'. Cheng (disapprovingly) quotes from Suzuki's

---

[7] See Richard H. Robinson, *Early Madhyamika in India and China* (Madison, Wisc.: University of Wisconsin Press, 1967), 57.

[8] Derrida's analysis of paradoxical formulations, and of other higher-order holisms (as distinguished from straightforward monism, say), belongs for the most part to his early phase. See, for example, "The Double Session" in his *Dissemination*, trans. B. Johnson (Chicago: University of Chicago Press, 1981), and "Differance" in his *Speech and Phenomena: And Other Essays on Husserl's Theory of Signs*, trans. D. B. Allison (Evanston, Ill.: Northwestern University Press, 1973), 134-5, 148-9.

[9] In Derrida the strict rigor of *ratio* undoes itself by being true to itself. I part company with Derrida in that I hold only mystical practice, a mysticism I call off-rational, can thoroughly attain deconstruction.

[10] Abe, ibid.

[11] See Derrida on Heidegger's version of *Durchstreichung* ('crossing-out') in "How to Avoid Speaking: Denials," trans. K. Frieden, in S. Budick and W. Iser, eds. *Languages of the Unsayable* (N.Y.: Columbia University Press, 1989), 56-7; Derrida goes on to deconstruct Heideggerian *Durchstreichung*, 58-62.

Outlines of Mahayana Buddhism, "Nāgārjuna's famous doctrine of 'the Middle Path of Eight No's' breathes the same (Upanishadic) spirit (Absolute Reality is to be described by No, No!)."[12] In my own work I usually follow the Prasangika-Madhyamika, which—unlike the Svatantrika-Madhyamika-Yogacara, does not regard the *Mūlamadhyamakakārikās* as inchoate.[13] The Prasangika-Madhyamika, and Candrakīrti (6th cent. C.E.) in particular, reduce their adversaries to *prasaṅga* ('absurd consequence') much like Derrida does in his own deconstructive practice,[14] and their understanding of *prajñapti* ('provisional language'/'conductal clue') approximates Derrida's *mise sous rature* ('placing under erasure'). From the Buddhist end of the Buddhist-Christian dialogue, the Prasangika-Madhyamika is best situated—I think—to heal the postmodern world.

This first section aims to show how 'pure negative reference' and several other 'misaligned' maneuvers 'work' in Derrida. This time I analyze a passage from *La Dissémination*,[15] a Derridean venue differing from those I have used before. (My treatment of Derrida's recent long essay "Dénégations," which has a relevance to 'pure negative reference' and religion,[16] I necessarily reserve for my current book-manuscript.)

---

[12] New York: Schocken Books, 1963, 102-3. Cited in Cheng, 121. Cheng is pointing out that Suzuki's version of Nāgārjuna's 'Eight Negations' makes them behave like a negative theology. That is, Suzuki's version assumes an Absolute Reality transcending the human attributions which the Eight Negations negate. Cheng would instead take the Eight Negations as a canceling-out of four dialectical (and therefore logocentric) opposites, such as, for example, 'annihilation' and 'permanence'. For him the Middle Path does not involve the negated pairs, but neither is there an Absolute which transcends them.

[13] For the distinctions between these two schools, a very good source is Jeffrey Hopkins, *Meditation on Emptiness* (London: Wisdom, 1983).

[14] That is, the Prasangika-Madhyamika, like Derrida, refuses to validate the position opposite to the absurd consequence.

[15] Jacques Derrida, *La Dissémination* (Paris: Seuil, 1972). Published English trans., B. Johnson (see note 8). Henceforth page references are supplied within brackets in the body of my text. The reference before the semicolon is to Johnson's trans., and after the semicolon, to the French original. In the case of a short quotation, I usually just supply the English pagination.

[16] I maintain that Derrida's "Comment ne pas parler—Dénégations" (French version, 1987) and the several pieces Derrida wrote in its wake, are reinscriptions/displacements of his earlier texts apropos of negative theology, and do not signal a concerted 'turn' in his thinking.

From Derrida's *La dissémination*:

> On ne peut donc pas se reposer dans la copule.[17] L'accouplement est le miroir. Le miroir se traverse *de lui-même*, autrement dit ne se traverse jamais. La traversée ne survient pas accidentellement au miroir—à l'Occident—elle est inscrite en sa structure. Autant dire que se produisant toujours, elle n'arrive jamais. Comme l'horizon. [353;392-3]

For analytic purposes, rather than the published English translation, I supply my more literal translation:

> One cannot, then, repose in the copula. Coupling is the mirror. The mirror is traversed *of/with/by itself* [se traverse *de lui-même*], which is to say that it is never traversed. The being-traversed does not come upon [ne survient pas...à: happen to] the mirror accidentally—in the West—it [the being-traversed] is inscribed in its structure. As much as to say, forever producing itself, it never comes to be (n'arrive jamais: never arrives]. Like the horizon.

This passage is part of a chapter deconstructing the verb *to be*, specifically in its philosophical use, the 'it is' (Latin: *est*; but also the French word *est*[18]) where ontology ('it is') is confounded with logico-mathematical equation (the = sign). From Derrida's deck I shall take only one cut, the argument—like Nāgārjuna's—which unconceals dilemma, and then opts for a debris-thesis X'd over. The formula of copula, A = B, is a fundament of much western thinking. But literally ('au pied de la lettre'), it is nonsensical. First horn of the dilemma: The = sign is traversed with no gain, "The mirror is traversed *of/with/by itself*," of its own accord. This is to say, if A = B, the A = B actually asserts A = A, a redundancy. Second horn of the dilemma: But a redundancy is to say the mirror really "is never traversed." If A = B, this is really to assert 'only A'. Two horns of a dilemma, both really asserting no more than that 'A *is not* B', A is *purely* not B. Pure negative reference. As for the third lemma, 'A both is and is not B', if posed in the undistributed sense,[19] it is here reducible to the

---

[17] Sexual coupling too. Throughout Derrida, there are potential analogies to be drawn to Tibetan Vajrayana in this regard.

[18] The *st* in French *est*, when *est* means the third person indicative of 'is', is not pronounced, allowing Derrida several highly instructive puns such as *écart* [*est quart*, *est cart(e)*], etc. And *est* is a French adverb meaning 'east' and noun meaning 'east' or 'East' (with these geographical meanings, the *st* is pronounced).

[19] In what is called technically the undistributed sense of the third lemma, 'Both A and not-A' means 'partly A and partly not-A', so that these two parts come together into a mathematical unity. In the distributed sense, 'both A and not-A' means 'both

first two lemmas (the same as in Nāgārjuna's *Mūla-*); and if posed in the distributed sense, it is considered irrational (the same as in Nāgārjuna's *Mūla-*).

In the same chapter, when dealing with the 'ontological' *est*, Derrida reiterates the strategy deployed against the 'logico-mathematical' *est*. "The 'is', which is 'Being' as an indication of presence, procures this [false] state of calm, this consciousness of ideal mastery...the column [of numbers, of print, of architecture, of the Bible's 'column of Fire', etc.] *is* this or that, *is there*; whether it is obvious or hidden behind the multiplicity of apparitions, the column is. But the column *has* no Being, nor any being-there, whether here or elsewhere" [352;391]. As much as to say, the *est* is never really traversed, A *is not* B, is never B. "The column *is not*, it is nothing but the passage of dissemination." The column is hollow, empty, "as transparent as the burning air in which the text carves out its path" [351;391]. The column is an abysmal square, an open cube with no top to cap it or bottom to hold it unless one *fantasizes* it either flat or a closed cube (whose closing surface can only be 'constructed' imaginatively, i.e., by mathematically 'cubing' the length of the side). The fantasized surface is logocentrism, the "mirror" which is the logical coupling we saw earlier (note that Derrida underscores the double-cross of ontology and numbers). Our excerpt continues:

> Et pourtant l'«est» qui a toujours voulu dire l'au-delà du narcissisme se prend dans le miroir. Lu dans l'écart, il n'arrive jamais. En tant qu'il est tourné vers l'«est», l'être se tient désormais sous cette rature comme quadrature. Il ne s'écrit que sous la grille des quatre fourches. [ibid, 393]

Here is my literal translation:

> And yet the *'est'* ['it is'; the East] which has always meant [voulu dire: Fr. locution from lit. *'wanted* to say'] what is beyond narcissism is caught in the mirror. Read in the fault/gap [écart: difference, deviation, digression, mistake, swerve, the 'discard' in cardgame, deviation, 'quarter' of a heraldric shield], it never arrives. Insofar as it is turned towards the *'est'* [the East; 'it is'], being confines itself [se tient: is held, sticks fast, contents itself] henceforth under this erasure [rature] like quadrature [quad*rature*: geom./astron. term—configuring of a square]. It is written only under the grid/grill/grille [grille: grid, grill, cloistered nuns' grille] of the four forks.

---

totally A and *totally* not-A', so that A and not-A come together into a paradoxical unity.

It should be clear enough that the *grille*, above, or *carrefour* ('crossroads') is not just nullification. In that ongoing doubling/doubled style so reminiscent of Ch'anist Buddhism's differential *kung-an*, Derrida has at least designed this passage to reveal/conceal that (1) a logocentric X nullifies and establishes, (2) a differential X (pure negative reference, here) negates and constitutes, and that (3) the logocentric and differential X's cut athwart each other, tangling each other up. In holistic terms a 'tangle' is of course read as a most unwelcome snag, a 'glitch'. But one of Derrida's most important contributions to 20th century thought is his showing wherein lies the *real* fecundity of logic (and here it is worthwhile recalling Derrida's steady commitment to the French rationalist tradition):—logic is at its best when, defense-mechanisms and pseudo-logical sleights of hand swept aside,[20] the thinker confronts logic-under-erasure, i.e., logic self-deconstructing (*not* self-destructing, mind you), and leaving the inevitable trace. A trace which is a logically inescapable snag or 'glitch'. And what is more/less, this trace is a *clue*: it is on-the-move.

Perforce, I limit myself to one zigzag through this 'passage', to show that the X is 'under erasure' but *conductal*. The traditional 'it is', thinking to escape the narcissism (cause and effect, signified and signifier, etc.), is caught precisely in the mirror of narcissism (the copula). Read in the empty square, it never traverses (i.e., it is in the condition of pure negative reference). Being, insofar as it is turned towards *logocentrism*, is unknowingly erased by its own logical assumptions, its own quadrature, the squaring which carries within itself its own undoing (logic undoing itself). Derrida is ALSO saying that Being, when turned towards the *East* (the Orient, off the east side of the page, etc.) is erased, quartered-up, put under the sign-of-quadrature, the sign of crossroads, the X. Given his celebration—via Sollers and otherwise—of the deconstructive traits of Chinese philosophy (they come from "the *other side* of the mirror,"[21] etc.), Derrida is here marking the not naive—let us say the X-wise—cutting-up of being, this *quartering*, as ORIENTAL.[22]

So Being is also written under the Oriental *grille*, the *grille* of difference, the *grille* of *is-not*. (But note, even in negating traditional logic,

---

[20] At least as much as possible.

[21] *Dissemination*, 356.

[22] But conversely, Derrida is also here satirizing anti-Oriental stereotypes, much as Edward Said does. And, obverse to this, he throughout this section deconstructs the *logocentric* tradition in the Orient (for of course the Orient has its 'centrisms', its logocentrisms, too).

logic must perforce in the same stroke erase this very gesture—pure negative erasure comes 'under the X' too). Notwithstanding, the Eastern *grille* purports a sort of LIBERATION from naiveté. [The good-humored off/allusions to food—the Messianic Banquet-Celebration to take place in the (Near-) East, etc., reinforce this note, though the Banquet is *not* treated as an attainable End.] Situational in its operation and plying the 'necessary but impossible' moment, the *est* which "ne s'écrit que sous la grille des quatre fourches" is here a Derridean *prajñapti* (in this Sanskrit term's second sense, 'conductal clue'). Derrida's *prajñapti* is a double-bind, so much so that even 'perversion' and mimicry, twisting in and up and over, subvert the ideal of an absolutely-defined *teleological* hope (e.g., western barbecue grill, the martyr's torture-grill, Chinese *grillade*, and the Eucharistic banquet-sacrifice,—these diverse senses here 'level-out' by way of 'mix-up').

The *prajñapti* is a double-bind: the DOUBLE-BIND is the *prajñapti* . It is 'conductal' to a sort of wisdom, and in Derrida not to a fulfillment (full-fill-ment) of a logocentric end, be that parousia or void. In the text entitled *La dissémination*, there is ongoing deconstruction of "the final parousia of a meaning at last deciphered, revealed…," deconstruction of "a truth past or a truth to come, to a meaning whose presence is announced by enigma" [350;389]. Instead, happenings issue as "altogether other" to each other yet as ongoing reinscriptions of "the same" ("Tout autre. La même") [366;407]. Always situational, the Derridean 'return of the same'—his version of Nāgārjuna's 'two truths' ('*saṁvṛti* is *paramārtha*'23) is well-exemplified in the chapter we have been treating. What Derrida situationally calls the "horizon-value" [351;390], that "pure infinite opening for the presentation of the present and the experience of meaning, here all at once it is framed [la voici tout à coup encadrée—the 'phenomenological moment', cf. *saṁvṛti*]. All at once it is a part [Et voici qu'elle fait partie]. And all at once apart [La voici partie— 'the devoid moment'—cf. *paramārtha*]. Thrown back into play [Elle est remise en jeu]."

Remark the "…expérience du sens, la voici encadrée tout à coup. Et voici qu'elle fait partie. La voici partie. Elle est remise en jeu." The "pure infinite [infinie: unfinished, unending, etc.] opening" and its perpetual framing and deframing are *on-the-move* ('on-the-move' without 'traversing'). "As soon as a sign emerges, it begins by repeating itself.

---

23 *Saṁvṛti* is the 'concealing truth', the mundane. *Paramārtha* is the 'supreme truth'. Nāgārjuna's unexpected and revolutionary stroke is to indicate the 'limits, realm' of *saṁvṛti* 'are' the 'limits, realm' of *paramārtha* .

Without this, it would not be a sign, would not be what it is,...the non-self-identity which regularly refers to the same. That is to say, to another sign, which itself will be born of having been divided."[24] Presence must "come to terms with [pure negative] relation...." It eventuates that this problematic "prevents there being *in fact* any difference between grammar and ontology."[25] When Derrida asserts that the ongoing alterity of happenings is "textual," is Writing, his strategy is to deconstruct the traditional notion that happenings are simply *logoi*, i.e., unities of meaning (analogically 'like' spoken words). Since for Derrida happenings are double-binds which move forward by the pure lack (the *is-not*) which is *negative overlap*,[26] happenings—including of course spoken words—are better understood *not* by a description of language-as-experienced[27] but by an analysis of how written signs really work-off/work. Otherwise put, spoken language better masquerades as self-identical, though such language too is necessarily in the double-bind: all talk is double-talk, and double-talk is double-bind (which is not at all to say, mark you, that all talk is outrightly untrue.) Derrida would say that all speaking and writing and thinking and doing are all Writing.

"The form of the chiasmus, the X," interests him, he says, "not as the symbol of the unknown but because there is here a sort of fork [the series *crossroads*, *quadrifurcum*, grid, grill, key, etc.] which is moreover unequal, one of its points extending its scope further than the other."[28] Further than the other so chiasmus can have a tilt to it, a tilt which necessarily engineers mobility, but a mobility which is somehow *neither* random *nor* purposeful. Both writing and Writing are as artificial as they are conventional, as much a question of free-play as of author's intention, of spatiality as temporality, etc., and suchwise that these moments criss-cross and undo each other, but always—please note—*unequally*. Disproportionately. Thus, the *overlap*. And always necessarily by pure *is not*. Thus the *negative* overlap.

---

[24] Derrida, *Writing and Difference*, trans. Alan Bass (Chicago: University of Chicago Press, 1978), 297.

[25] *Dissemination*, 166.

[26] See *Dissemination*, 304.

[27] In other words, not by *phenomenology*.

[28] Derrida seems to have in mind the calligraphic form of the Greek *chi*, wherein the left-to-right downstroke is normally longer than the right-to-left second stroke. For this quotation (itself a citation from Derrida's *Positions*), see Derrida, *The Truth in Painting*, trans. Geoff Bennington and Ian McLeod (Chicago: University of Chicago Press, 1987), 166.

In reprise, we can say that writing is a *prajñapti* for Writing, and Writing in Derrida means the ongoing alterity of happenings.[29] It falls to me to rewrite the foregoing with a furthermore, the more and no more that Derrida's Writing is a *prajñapti* for Nāgārjuna's *pratītya samutpāda*, 'dependent-arising'.[30] Like the 'dependent-arising' in the *Mūlamadhyamakakārikās*, Writing is dependence-only, and thus is never a totality, never a whole (Derrida: "The supplement is always unfolding, but it can never attain the status of a complement [and thus consummate the whole]. The field is never saturated"[31]). Like 'dependent-arising', which is *marked, discontinuous* (each 'moment' purely different) yet the 'same' (pure negative relation as constitutive: constitutive of the 'sameness without self-identity'), Derrida's Writing is purely different yet the 'same'.

Mark what Derrida says about the series of marks, what he calls in one situation a series of *traces*, and in another the *tr-* (as in "travail in train, trait, traject, in-trigue," but it could be just as well a *gl-* or an *fr-* or an x[32]: how to act-out, how to *signature*, that which is off-nameable, i.e., that which is not a unity?). Derrida says, in a 'reinscribed' figure, 'forever recurring' in his *t*reatment of Adami,[33] that the marks on march, the traces, the *tr-*, whose "so-called whole words are different each time in form and content," the *tr-* which is "not a self-identity, [not] a proper meaning or body,"[34] *are* at once "the *same* mutation."[35] That which "only holds together...by having nothing to do with"[36] is like "double scale ['scale' = *échelle*], double measure, and yet the *same, one* ladder ['ladder' also = *échelle* in French]."[37] "Thus works, in or outside language, a *tr–*."[38] (Even the theologian David *Tracy* carries the *trace* of it, one might

---

[29] See Derrida, *D'Un ton apocalyptique adopté naguère en philosophie* (Paris: Galilée, 1983), 85; Derrida, "Living on: *Border Lines*," in *Deconstruction and Criticism*, Harold Bloom et al. (N.Y.: Continuum, 1984), 96-7; *Writing and Difference*, 296; and *Dissemination*, 351, 366.

[30] For the etymology of this term, which has been much controverted in Buddhist history, see J. Hopkins, 161–73.

[31] Derrida, "White Mythology: Metaphor in the Text of Philosophy," trans. F. C. T. Moore, in *New Literary History*, 6, 1 (1974), 18.

[32] See *Truth in Painting*, 169.

[33] See *Truth in Painting*, 149-182.

[34] Nor a question of a "semantic nucleus" such as *trans-* or *tra-*, of course. See *Truth in Painting*, 171.

[35] Emphasis mine. See *Truth in Painting*, 181.

[36] *Truth in Painting*, 174.

[37] *Truth in Painting*, 166, my emphasis.

[38] *Truth in Painting*, 173.

say.) Which I *t*ranscribe, 'THUS works, in or outside writing/speaking, a Writing'. Dependently arising.

This second section of my paper tries to show how 'pure negative reference' and some other maneuvers treated in Derrida's texts can help Christians better understand the Trinity and Unity of God. My call for quite some time has been that Christianity can only learn from dialogue with other religions if it learns to find what in them is 'other'. Masao Abe, with the best of intentions, has proffered to Christian theologians what he considers a more suitable model than their traditional one(s) for thinking about God. If Christians 'dialogue' with Abe's proposal that God is a Dynamic Nothingness originating identity-and-difference by way of absolute *kenōsis*, they are—perhaps unconsciously—targeting in this Buddhist's presentation that with which they are *already most comfortable* (so as to make of it 'more of the same'). For, despite the complex doctrinal differences which may render even Abe's suggested thesis 'unorthodox' (in historical Western terms), Christianity has been familiar with its paradoxical model and even its rhetoric for a long time.

That God is better served by the formula of 'A is not-A' appears (for example) in one form or another in the work of the Dionysian tradition from Pseudo-Dionysius down through Eckhart, Tauler, Suso, Ruysbroeck, and Boehme. In the final analysis, a Dynamic Nothingness as Abe presents it is still holistic, paradoxically transcendent and immanent, infinite yet within-a-frame. In the final analysis, then, still *safe and comfortable* for traditional Western discourse about God. What I have long contended is that Christianity must learn (and 'test', as St. Paul says[39]) that which is 'uncomfortable'. For example, that 'God'—as Raimundo Panikkar and Karl Rahner remind us[40]—is impersonal as well as personal. Indeed, that 'God' is sometimes frighteningly *impersonal* and that this *impersonality* double-binds into Divine *personality* in erratic, ever-altering ways that *do not* close into unity. (Which, by the way, is not at all to say that God is not a *loving* God.) That such a God is not encompassed, is not *captured* by either the formula or experience of a 'unifying source' *is* unsettling, *is* frightening for most Christians. All the more reason why

---

[39] 1 Thessalonians 5:21.
[40] See R. Panikkar, *The Trinity and the Religious Experience of Man* (N.Y.: Orbis, 1973), 50, 64, 68-9; also 19, 38-9, 52-5. For the Rahnerian school's claim that humanity is united to God precisely because of God's difference from human 'personality' (a 'difference' enabled by the Divine difference within God), see Elmar Klinger, in Karl Rahner, ed., with C. Ernst and K. Smith, *Sacramentum Mundi*, Vol. 4 (N.Y.: Herder and Herder, 1968), 95.

it is differential Madhyamika Buddhism which can most serviceably witness to Christians in dialogue, as should happen, for example, when a Christian meets the rNying-ma-pa's (Tibetan) Madhyamika critique of the 'mentalist' (Tibetan) Yogacara:

> The difference between the mentalistic and Madhyamika systems is that the former locates this mistakenness in not recognizing a purely luminous (*gsal*) and congnitive (*rig*) noetic capacity (*shes-pa*) which is beyond the subject-object dichotomy (*gzung,'dzin*), as the source of experience; while the latter reject even this noetic capacity as as much a postulate as that of a corresponding external object.[41]

No undeconstructed 'source' for these Madhyamikans. Surely we should not expect that Christianity's deconstruction of holism *imitate* Buddhist deconstruction. Indeed, the very thesis of this paper, when applied to Buddhist-Christian dialogue, means that the two religions erect their 'sameness' by way of their very differences. What I have found, rather, is that 'pure negative reference' has been 'crypted' into Christian theology for a long time, perhaps from the beginning. Crypted into Christian theology in ways purely differing from the Buddhist ones. For me the topic of Buddhist-Christian dialogue in this paper becomes, then, an intersection of Buddhist devoidness and Christian devoidness, two intersecting lines that necessarily have no 'common ground'.

The cipher to/of 'pure negative reference' is secreted in a place some would deem most unlikely (especially since its results prove to be 'postmodern'), namely, Christian Conciliar theology. Designed for other *ad hoc* reasons, the cipher has never really been decoded in terms of devoidness. And because of its traditional provenance, nowadays it is largely ignored (the word GK *kruptos*, 'hidden', makes not only the word 'crypto[gram]' in English, but also 'crypt', after all). But let us agree, at least provisionally, to try useful ideas when/where we can, whether they come by serendipity or whatever. For prejudice exhibits a most craven craving.

It was the Council of Florence (1438-9 C.E.) that affirmed "everything is one" in God, "except where an opposition of relationship [*relationis oppositio*] exists,"[42] so that each of the three Persons *as* a Person is constituted (i.e., defined, established) *only* by oppositional relations

---

[41] Kennard Lipman, "Introduction" to Klong-chen-pa, trans. K. Lipman, *Yid-bzhin rin-po-che'i mdzod*, in *Crystal Mirror*, 345–6.
[42] Karl Rahner's adroit translation, in Rahner, "Divine Trinity," *Sacramentum Mundi*, Vol. 6, 298.

among the Persons. Most theologians have always taken *relationis oppositio* in the Thomist sense (though this is by no means strictly necessary for the case I am making), namely—the 'opposition of relation' is *contrariety* rather than *contradiction*.[43] (The relation between black and white, for example, is an opposition of contrariety, whereas the relation between black and non-black is an opposition of contradiction.) The only 'functions' that are applied *uniquely* to the Father, Son, and Holy Spirit *respectively* in Scripture are the following: 'Paternity' to the Father, 'Filiation' (Sonship) to the Son, and 'Passive Spiration' (That which is 'breathed-out') to the Holy Spirit.

That such is the case becomes one of the reasons, apparently, why Karl Rahner rejects the 'psychological' theory of Trinity associated (among his contemporaries) with Bernard Lonergan. Conciliar theologians who define the Father as the Knower, for example, and the Son as the Known (i.e., 'Truth'), seem to ignore that Scripture in one place or another identifies Knowing with (in this case) each of the three Persons all told. Which is to say, according to the *relationis oppositio* clause, that Knowing (in our example) does not define the Persons at all, but the Unity of God *instead*. (Scripture's attribution of Knowing, then, to any one Person at any one time is said to be just 'appropriated' to the Person: it does not *really* belong to that unique Person.)

If one considers this operation carefully, it is mind-bending in a very wonderful and 'postmodern' way. *All* that the Persons would share is sacrificed, is preempted, is always already 'gutted out' of them, so that it belongs to the Unity. This 'syncopation' in the midst of God is *kenōsis*, certainly, but—since the Personal contrarieties 'remain'—it is 'devoid' *kenōsis* (and not the 'void' *kenōsis* of Abe's model). Furthermore, we should speak of *kenōses* (plural) rather than *kenōsis*, since the 'opposition of relation' between Paternity and Filiation, say, is not the same as that between Active Spiration and Passive Spiration, and thus what is preempted out of them is not the same. (As for the special problematic of Spiration, we shall address it in a moment.) Finally, apropos of the Personal contraries, there is at least one other point to be noted here. Namely, while it is the case the *kenōses* are devoid, Persons relate contrariwise in terms of *pure negative reference*. Somehow the Father (for

---

[43] See Edmund Fortman, *The Triune God: A Historical Study of the Doctrine of the Trinity* (London and Philadelphia: Hutchinson/Westminster, 1972), 222-23. In this matter, for a more finessed treatment of contrariety and contradictory than I can give in this paper, see *Derrida on the Mend*, 146-7.

example) *is purely not* the Son (recall that what they 'would' share has instead gone over to the Unity).

In the model of the Triune God Masao Abe proposes for Christians, the "oneness of the one God must possess the characteristic of zero" (absolute *kenōsis*: here in fact Abe uses the traditional German term *Ungrund*) in order that "Trinity be fully and dynamically realized...three distinctive beings—Father, Son, and Spirit—are then clearly and thoroughly realized in their distinctiveness....[44] The originating unity of God is absolute emptying-out (*Ungrund*, or '-A'), and thus paradoxically concretizes the three Persons (Persons, or '+A'). The model of the Triune God proposed by Conciliar theology stands in sharp contrast. Its *relationis oppositio* clause limns a Trinity that works converse to Abe's model, in that the three Persons raise the 'sameness' of the Unity by way of *their* emptyings-out; and crosswise to Abe's model in that the 'lateral' contraries (of the Persons) constitute the Unity *indirectly*, that is, by default, and the contrary relations are themselves 'pure negative references'. The *kenōses* raising the Divine Unity are devoid, and the Unity and the Three Persons are *not* interchangeable. Masao Abe's model, on the other hand, is strictly holistic: it postulates an absolute and direct *kenōsis* , and the interchangeability of Unity and Trinity (-A = +A).

As promised, I now turn to the problematic of the Holy Spirit and its 'procession' (*Processio*) from the Father and/through[45] the Son. The Holy Spirit is said to proceed from the Father/Son "as from one principle."[46] Given that even in (what is called) the Eastern Church's formula (i.e., "through the Son"), it is not a question of the Father *transferring* Himself or a part of Himself to or through the Son (this would vitiate the *relationis oppositio* clause), the question opens up,—How does the 'one principle' work? I have argued elsewhere that the Derridean deconstruction of Signifier-Signified dyads can supply us with a clue in this regard.[47] The relevant citation from Derrida is the following:

> In this play of representation, the point of origin becomes ungraspable. There are things like reflecting pools, and images, an infinite reference from one to the other, but no longer a source/spring [source]. There is no longer simple origin. For what is reflected is split *in itself* and not only as an

[44] Abe, 24.
[45] At the Council of Florence, both the formula of the Western Church ("from the Father and the Son") and the Eastern Church ("from the Father through the Son") are confirmed.
[46] Second Council of Lyons (1271-6 C.E.).
[47] See *Derrida on the Mend*, 134-44; also 9-20.

addition to itself of its image. The reflection, the image, the double, splits what it doubles [le double dédouble ce qu'il redouble]....and the law of addition of the origin to its representation, of the thing to its image, is that one plus one make at least three.[48]

The representation, or Signifier, boomerangs back as *different* from the Signified, and therefore as *its* cause (while the Signified *also* remains as cause), so the model of simple dyad breaks down. Or, to conceive of this action from the other end, as Derrida did for us earlier in this paper, the Signified is "caught in the mirror" and "never arrives." Instead, it is split there in the mirror.

Either way, the "addition" of the Third requires the interaction of what we called the 'initial' Signified and Signifier; and requires that the interaction involve infringement. I use the word 'initial' advisedly, because what we are doing is, after all, a *deconstruction*. That is to say, we are learning/showing 'sequentially' where the traditional logic of Signification *really* must lead, if one doesn't flinch and fudge. I use the word 'infringement' advisedly, because the Signifier usurps the causality belonging to the Signified. What we learn from the deconstruction is that the Signified-Signifier dyad is *'always already'* three, and that the Third of these three proceeds perpetually from a transgressive yet singular interaction of the other two. And we learn finally that this 'alternative solution', the workings of the two that are three, must also necessarily come *sous rature*, "under the grid of the *four* forks."

I argue that this Signified-Signifier dyad Which-is-always-already-Three operates as the best clue (towards understanding the *Processio*) that 20th century philosophy has hatched.[49] The Derridean account would indicate how the Father and Son infringe each other and still 'as one principle' spirate the Holy Spirit. As we have just seen, Derrida's Signified and Signifier so split as to make a Third, and a split is of course disruption. 'Disruption' in the sense that the Signifier does not at all close around into the Signified (does not do so even though this 'circle' is conventionally expected, indeed, *most* expected). In short, the Signifier

---

[48] Derrida, trans. G. Spivak, *Of Grammatology* (Baltimore: Johns Hopkins, 1976), 36. French edition, *De la Grammatologie* (Paris: Minuit, 1967), 54-5.

[49] 'To hatch: v.t. 1. To produce from an egg or eggs.... 2. To produce. v.i. 1. To produce young'.

'To hatch: v.t. 1. To mark with hatching.'

'To crosshatch: v.t. & i. To mark with series of parallel lines that cross, especially obliquely'.

does not somehow *mediate* the Signified. And in Conciliar theology it turns out that a like 'disruption' is necessarily in effect.

The theology strictly distinguishes between the 'one principle' that spirates the Holy Spirit and the Father's *Generatio* that begets the Son. The *Generatio* is unilateral (the Son cannot beget the Father in turn) but the 'aspiration from one principle' involves the Father and Son in a kind of mutual transgression,[50] in a kind of *disruption*. Which is to say, in short, that there is no *mediation* between them. The Holy Spirit proceeds "from the Father and *at once* from the Son, and *from both* eternally as from one principle" ("...ex Patre *simul et* Filio, et *ex utroque* aeternaliter tamquam ab uno principio"). Even in what is called the Eastern formula, "ex Patre per Filium, "from the Father through the Son," any 'mediation' as such is excluded: "the Son, also, is according to the Greeks indeed the cause, according to the Latins indeed the principle" of the Procession, "and the Father is too" ("Filius quoque esse secundum Graecos quidem causam, secundum Latinos vero principium...sicut et Patrem"[51]). All the while remaining 'one cause/principle', the Son is considered the cause/principle and the Father is considered the cause/principle.

Next, there is a wonderfully Divine *'glitch'* in the Conciliar theology of the Triune God. Given that the 'one principle' of Father and/through Son is in 'oppositional relation' to the Holy Spirit it establishes, the 'one principle' would appear to be a *fourth* Person. But a fourth Person is deemed Biblically impossible. Thus theology has long insisted that this Active Spiration (of Father and/through Son) which 'breathes out' the Holy Spirit (Who is the Passive Spiration) is *virtual*, not real.[52] ('Virtual' is taken to mean 'of only functional validity'.) But the Councils have long said the Passive Spiration, on its side, is *real*. Otherwise, the Holy Spirit would not be real, and thus not a Person. The equivocating status of the Active Spiration has long exercised the problem-solving temper of speculative theologians. I think, however, that the equivocating status

---

[50] In the literal sense, i.e., the Father and Son 'go across' each other's (logocentrically expected) 'defining borders'. By 'infringement', 'transgression', 'disruption', I do not imply hostile action, needless (perhaps) to say, but rather a breaking across logocentric definitions.

[51] *Enchiridion symbolorum definitionum et declarationum* (Rome, Barcelona, New York, Freiburg i. Br.: Herder, 34th ed. 1967), Council of Florence DZ 691.

[52] See Karl Rahner, *The Trinity*, trans. J. Donceel (N.Y.: Seabury, 1974), 77-8; and Edmund Fortman, 293-4.

works more like a Derridean double-bind,[53] and is very fruitful when taken as such. Written "under the grid of the four forks," it becomes Divine trace, and conductal towards the *mystērion* of the Triune God.

The Active Spiration as Double-Bind. To wit:—(1) The Active Spiration *overlaps* with the definition of a Divine Person because it is in oppositional relation (*relationis oppositio*) to the Third Person, the Holy Spirit, and thus would be a Person too, but (First Bind) this is *negative overlap* because the Active Spiration is virtual, not real, and thus *not* a Person. (2) The Active Spiration *overlaps* with the definition of the Divine Unity because 'as one principle' the Father and/through the Son are transgressive of each other but are *not* oppositional to each other, and "everything is one in God except where *relationis oppositio* exists," but (Second Bind) this is *negative overlap* because the 'one principle' *cannot* belong to the Unity: it is locked instead into a singular *oppositional* relation with the Holy Spirit, who is a real Person. (X) The Active Spiration, as *neither* Personhood *nor* Divine Unity, is thus a privileged clue to the Difference between them. That is, to the Difference 'within' the Triune God. Somehow, in negative overlaps and nonholistically does the happening of God perpetually go-on.

Karl Rahner and Raimundo Panikkar remind us that Christians still need a theology of the 'impersonal' in God. The problem is compounded when we remember that even the term 'Person' in Trinitarian theology does not mean 'person' in the human sense of the word. The Greek term *hypostasis* was meant by the Council theologians to avoid twin fallacies: that the Trinity involved a 'modal variation of the Divine Unity' on the one hand, or an 'anthropomorphic personhood' on the other.[54] If we go on to distinguish between the terms 'Person' (as in the Trinity) and 'person' (as in human personhood), differential theology can assert (1) the Divine Unity is devoid and imPersonal, (2) the Trinity—because of its internal voiding oppositions—is Personal, and (3) the Triune God is 'impersonal' (except for the Son, insofar as the Son is incarnate in Jesus Christ, who in His human nature has 'personal consciousness'). What is more/less, this formulation of the Triune God undergoes dislocation by way of the Divine Glitch addressed earlier, so that God becomes—for those demanding a God of 'stable definition'—quite frightening indeed.

---

[53] That Derridean double-binds are not paradoxical should be clear: the binds are not congruent with each other, nor do they somehow compose a whole. See Derrida's commentary/demonstration in *The Truth in Painting*, 162.
[54] *Nor* does it involve human *gender*, of course.

(All the more so, still, if one recalls that this Glitch is just a paltry clue—it too comes under erasure, and, needless to say, God's own erasure.)

The semantic pair 'personal-impersonal' opens up a third sense as well, whereby 'impersonal' connotes 'not-caring', 'not-loving', etc. The Biblical tradition reveals almighty God to be Lover of humanity and performer of Loving deeds (culminating with Love on the cross), and thereby teaches Christians that God is radically *not* 'impersonal' in the human pejorative sense. But my point here is that God is 'personal' *and* 'impersonal', and this latter, this 'more-than-personal', can easily appear to humans as non-Loving. What differential theology does is confirm what many Christian mystics (and other mystics) have attested, that God—while still imbricated into us—is nonetheless radically *otherwise* ("neither are your ways my ways," Isa. 55:8; "how inscrutable his ways," Rom. 11:33).

No doubt the reports of mystics belonging to the 'centric' tradition later recast this Otherwise into familiar logocentric formulae, but others most certainly do not.[55] For the differential mystics, the Burning Bush, unquenchable, is all afire for sure, but all *atangle* at the same time. In particular these mystics report how God has to shock them into the Divine Otherwise. Differential theology, for its part, suggests that the 'unchanging God' is the God of Same, not the Self-Same. And that God is better served by the notion of alterity than stasis. The Same of the Divine Unity then becomes more like an ever-roaming (MF *errant*) Sameness, an infinite Repetition-with-a-drift. And this Divine Unity is raised by Personal (trinitarian) *kenōses* which ever differ, forever. Like a truly Infinite Retreat of emptyings-out. And this Triune God would seem to loop forever from the elegant double-bind at Its (unwedged) core.

Healing becomes, then, not a question of holism but of sameness established by difference. In Christianity, even when Christ prays "that all may be one, as you Father in me, and I in you" (John 17:21), the point would be that *as* the Father and Son purely differ and so establish their oneness, *so* (by differing) shall "all be one." And in Madhyamikan Buddhism too (as we saw), where the *explanation* of difference differs so dramatically from the Christian explanation, the constituted sameness works all the more by way of negative reference, indeed—in the Madhyamikan Buddhist case—a purely negative reference without exception.

---

[55] For an example of a Christian mystic who is not centric, read Derrida on Angelus Silesius in Derrida, "Post-Scriptum: Aporias, Ways and Voices," in H. Coward and T. Foshay, eds., *Derrida and Negative Theology*, (Albany: SUNY Press, 1992), 282-323.

Intersections are lines. Lines have no 'space', no 'dimension', so they cannot have ground 'in common'. Let us calmly agree to disagree. The devoidnesses of Buddhism, and Christianity, and Derridean deconstruction (and of others too)—while/as intersecting—are by this very fact *apart*. The 'samenesses' they thus constitute shall heal the world.

Notes on Contributors

Philippa Berry is a fellow of King's College, University of Cambridge, where she lectures in English. She is the author of *Of Chastity and Power: Elizabethan literature and the unmarried queen* (Routledge 1989), and the editor, with Andrew Wernick, of *Shadow of Spirit: Postmodernism and Religion* (Routledge 1992). She is currently working on two books: *Dying with a Difference: the body of woman in Shakespeare's tragedies* (forthcoming from Routledge), and a contribution to feminist theory provisionally entitled *Dancing in Space*. A student of the mystical traditions of both East and West, she is committed to the integration of intellectual work with spiritual practice.

Roger Corless is professor of Religion at Duke University. He studied theology at King's College, University of London and Buddhism at the University of Wisconsin in Madison. His publications include books on Christian meditation and articles on Pure Land Buddhism and Buddhist-Christian studies. Baptized and confirmed in the Roman Catholic Church, and having taken refuge with a lama of the Tibetan Buddhist Gelugpa lineage, he is attempting to be a focus for both Buddhist and Christian practice, and to write out of that experience.

Morny Joy is associate professor in the Religious Studies department of the University of Calgary, where she teaches philosophy of religion and comparative philosophy. She studied hermeneutics with Paul Ricoeur and her recent publications include "Conclusion: Divine Reservations" in *Derrida and Negative Theology* (SUNY 1992), "Equality or Divinity: A False Dichotomy" *Journal of Feminist Studies in Religion* 6 (4) 1990, "Derrida and Ricoeur: A Case of Mistaken Identity and Difference" *Journal of Religion* 68 (4) 1988, and "Rhetoric and Hermeneutics" *Philosophy Today* 32 (4) 1988.

David Loy is professor in the Faculty of International Studies, Bunkyo University, Chigasaki 253, Japan. He is the author of *Nonduality: a study in comparative philosophy* (Yale 1988), *Lack and Transcendence: the problem of death and life in psychotherapy, existentialism and Buddhism* (Humanities Press 1996), "The Deconstruction of Buddhism" in *Derrida and Negative Theology* (SUNY 1992), and various journal articles. Raised as a Roman Catholic, he is a longtime student of Zen.

Robert Magliola, now professor of philosophy and religious studies at Abac University in Thailand, is professor emeritus of National Taiwan University, where he was Distinguished Chair professor in its Graduate School. He is the author of *Phenomenology and Literature* (Purdue 1977; 1978) and *Derrida on the Mend* (Purdue 1984; 1986) and many book chapters. His next book is entitled *Crosshatching the Pervasive Buddha*. A Carmelite tertiary, he practiced Ch'an/Zen meditation for 22 years, and is now training as an 8-precept layman at Wat Mahathat, Bangkok. He organized the panel on "Healing Deconstruction" at the Fourth International Buddhist-Christian Dialogue Conference (Boston University, July-August 1992) where earlier versions of this book's papers were presented.